WARS OF THE THIRD KIND

WARS OF THE THIRD KIND: CONFLICT IN UNDERDEVELOPED COUNTRIES

Edward E. Rice

UNIVERSITY OF CALIFORNIA PRESS

Berkeley   Los Angeles   London

University of California Press
Berkeley and Los Angeles, California
University of California Press, Ltd.
London, England
© 1988 by
The Regents of the University of California

Library of Congress Cataloging-in-Publication Data

Rice, Edward E. (Edward Earl), 1909–
  Wars of the third kind : conflict in under-
developed countries / Edward E. Rice.
      p.   cm.
  Bibliography: p.
  Includes index.
  ISBN 0-520-06236-1 (alk. paper)
    1. Developing countries—History, Military.
2. Guerrilla warfare—History.   3. World politics.
I. Title.
D883.R53   1988
909'.09724—dc19   87-30894
                                      CIP

Printed in the United States of America
1   2   3   4   5   6   7   8   9

Contents

For countries as for people, there can be few surer prescriptions for disaster than commitment to an undertaking that is inadequately understood and from which there seems to be no turning back. Because it takes two to make peace, but only one to make war, and because pride inhibits the admission of gross error, wars are undertakings from which extrication is peculiarly difficult. There is widespread understanding of conventional wars as they have been fought among the modern powers, and there is enough knowledge of nuclear war—if something so apocalyptic can be called war—to tell us that it must be prevented. There are, however, wars of another, or third, kind, neither nuclear nor conventional, to which a major power may become almost inadvertently committed. Because of the reliance of one side on hit-and-run operations, these conflicts are usually called *guerrilla wars*. The term, however, is incompletely descriptive: the reliance of the one side on guerrilla operations may be only partial; it may over time gain the capacity to wage battles of position and maneuver; and its opponent may attempt throughout the conflict to fight a conventional war. Accordingly, a more appropriate designation for such conflicts might be *wars of the third kind*.

The disparities in strength between great powers and less developed lands, and between regular armies and guerrilla bands, have commonly led civilian and military leaders to predict that wars of the third kind upon which they embark will be short and easily won. But the reverse has almost invariably been the case. In 1774 George III, having decided that the American colonies should be reduced to obedience, predicted that "once these rebels have felt a smart blow, they will submit." Seven years of exchanging blows provided the measure of his miscalculation. In 1808 Napoleon invaded economically backward Spain in what was intended to be a war of quick decision. It too lasted seven years; it cost Napoleon half a million men he could ill afford to lose; and it introduced into English the Spanish word *guerrilla*. In the latter part of 1899 General Elwell S. Otis was telling American correspondents in Manila that the conflict we call the Philippine Insurrection was over; actually, its guerrilla phase had just begun and would last for upward of five years. In December 1946 Chiang Kai-shek expressed to General George C. Marshall his confidence that he could exterminate the forces of the Chinese Communists in a matter of months; less than three years later, all mainland China was in their hands. The list of such cases might be extended indefinitely, and it would be hard to find the exception that is supposed to confirm the rule.

In 1962, with his eyes on the growing American involvement in Vietnam, President Kennedy declared that guerrilla wars required "a whole new kind of strategy, a wholly different kind of force, and therefore a new and wholly different kind of military training."[1] (In this view he was contradicted by the Army chief of staff, who asserted that "any good soldier can handle guerrillas.")[2] Six years later, after the United States had decided to hold peace talks with North Vietnam, Henry Kissinger in effect declared that no such strategy had been found. The strategies we had brought to the Vietnam conflict had been failures, he said, and if we were to avoid similar disasters, which might look quite different but would embody the same essentials, we would have to reassess the ideas that got us involved there.[3]

It cannot be expected that a conceptual study relevant to such wars—wars that in essence are the same, however much they may differ in their particulars—will be made by a high government official. In general, the higher the official, the wider the range of matters with which he or she is concerned, and breadth implies a sacrifice of depth. During my own government service, spent below those echelons, I had unusual opportunities to observe and consider conflicts in which guerrilla operations played a substantial role. Because that service provided the foundation for my further study of the subject, leading to the writing of this book, it is owing to the reader to provide a brief account of it.

I spent the eight years between the outbreak of the Sino-Japanese War in 1937 and the end of World War II in 1945 in China as a Foreign Service officer with Chinese language and area training. During the first half of that period, I was stationed successively in three cities when they were taken over by Japanese forces—Peking, Canton, and Foochow—and experienced a fourth occupation when the Japanese evacuated Foochow and it was retaken by the Chinese. Accordingly, what I first witnessed were conventional military operations viewed chiefly from the vantage point of urban centers, and when I first heard claims being made for the effectiveness of the guerrilla warfare being conducted by the Chinese Communists behind the Japanese lines I received them with disbelief.

I was at that time serving in Chungking, the wartime capital, but in 1943 I began a two-year assignment as a reporting officer on detached service in a region just south of the communist area centered at Yenan and immediately west of the Japanese lines. While on this assignment I learned that the Communists' armed formations and political cadres had indeed gained control—at the expense of both stay-behind nationalist forces, which were no match for them, and the invading Japanese—over wide areas of North China. During those years I was able to gauge the performance of both Chinese communist and nationalist forces against the Japanese, and also against each other. I had for some time believed that the end of World War II would be followed by the resumption of China's nationalist-communist civil war, and I now became convinced the Nationalists would not win it. I also began to fear that the Chinese Nationalists, who had done little fighting against the Japanese since our entry into the war in 1941, would continue to look to us for help against their communist enemies, and that we might become disastrously involved. I could not, however, foresee how many years would pass before we put that possibility behind us.

In August 1945, with the surrender of Japan, I was ordered to proceed to Washington on transfer to the Department of State, and the first leg of my journey took me back to Chungking. While there I paid a call on Major General Patrick J. Hurley, who had been appointed ambassador to China late the previous year. I had heard little about him except that he cut a most handsome figure, dominated conversations with practiced facility, and liked when elated to let out war whoops, a practice perhaps related to his having grown up in Oklahoma when it was Indian territory. General Hurley had been sent to China with the missions of harmonizing relations between Generalissimo Chiang Kai-shek and General Joseph W. Stilwell, commander of the U.S. forces in China, and of bringing about the unification of the military forces of China in the interests of the war against Japan. The Chinese quickly convinced Hurley that Stilwell had to go, and he was replaced by General Albert C. Wedemeyer, whom Chiang found much more amenable. Nominally, Chinese communist forces had been a part of the government's military establishment since 1937—they had been given government unit designations and their commander in chief had accepted a government appointment. But a truly unified command could only be established as part of a political settlement. General Hurley had tried to bring about such a settlement and it had thus far eluded him, but he was continuing his efforts because without a settlement there would be a renewal of civil war.

While discussing his problems during my call, General Hurley expressed the belief that the Chinese Communists were not truly Communists—a view with which I was prepared to dissent, had he given me the opportunity. The main difference between them and his fellow Republicans back in Oklahoma, he declared, was that the Chinese Communists were armed. Hurley nevertheless made it clear that he conceived it to be U.S. policy to support the Nationalists against the Communists. The Communists were at that point attempting to assert the right to participate in taking the Japanese surrender, and Hurley declared with evident satisfaction that any Japanese troops who surrendered their weapons to communist units would be required to go get them back. As he rose from his chair and began to accompany me to the door, he related—perhaps to convince me of his determination—an account of an engagement during World War I in which a large proportion of his command had become casualties, but that had ended with him still holding his ground.

At that point there were about sixty thousand American servicemen in China, many of them carrying out a U.S. commitment to train and equip thirty-nine divisions of Chinese troops and an air force of eight and one third groups. U.S. forces also were beginning the task of assisting the Chinese government to reoccupy Japanese-held areas of China by providing airlift and sealift to East and North China for some half a million nationalist troops. In addition, about fifty thousand U.S. marines were landed in North China, where they took responsibility for keeping rail lines in operation and repatriating Japanese troops and civilians. The instructions under which they operated called for their avoiding involvement in Chinese civil strife, but with clashes occurring as a result of nationalist troops being transported into communist-held areas of North China and Manchuria, such involvement was sometimes unavoidable.

Such was the situation in China in the autumn of 1945 when I began what was to be a three-year assignment in the State Department's Division of Chinese Affairs. General Hurley had come to Washington on consultation in September, and toward the end of November, instead of returning to China, he abruptly sent President Truman a letter of resignation. The president then appointed General George C. Marshall to serve as his special representative in China entrusted with promoting the peaceful settlement between the two Chinese sides that had eluded General Hurley. I thought Marshall's mission was doomed from the start, inasmuch as I was convinced that the differences between the Nationalists and the Communists were irreconcilable. Like oil and water shaken together, it seemed for a time that they might be successfully combined, but a cease-fire agreement reached in January 1946 was never really kept. Negotiations broke down, and after a year's effort Marshall came home to assume the position of secretary of state. Viewed solely in the context of its announced purpose, Marshall's mission had been a failure, but seen from a broader standpoint, it was not without important accomplishments. It had gained the time needed for the bulk of U.S. military personnel in China to complete their tasks and come home, without becoming seriously involved in that country's civil war.

In the Department of State, the officers of the Division of Chinese Affairs did not learn of the decision to send General Marshall to China until it was announced by the White House. This struck me at the time as extraordinary, but I was later to realize that at the highest level in Washington, where the most important decisions are reached, the number of those participating is likely to be the smallest. Moreover, had I been consulted, I would not have been able to demonstrate that the Marshall Mission would be unable to achieve its announced purpose, for I reached that conclusion through an intuition born of numerous inputs, many of which would have been beyond conscious recall. (I subsequently was interested to learn, in this general connection, that Dean Acheson, while secretary of state, had great difficulty in accepting some of the recommendations of such eminent Foreign Service officers as George Kennan and Charles Bohlen because they had not been reached through a consciously formulated series of steps. What Acheson needed in his dealings with the president was communicable wisdom, rather than mere conclusions, however soundly based in experience or intuition.[4] This, I suspect, is a problem that will often characterize relations between career Foreign Service officers and the politically appointed officials under whom they serve.)

General Marshall assumed his new responsibilities early in 1947, and during the first six months of his incumbency, the tide of battle in the Chinese civil war turned against the Nationalists. The Chinese government had begun the civil war with an estimated five-to-one superiority in combat troops and rifles, a virtual monopoly of heavy equipment and transport, and an unopposed air arm.[5] It had been provided with the assistance of a joint U.S. military advisory group; large quantities of arms and ammunition, much of it gratis; Lend–Lease aid; and

Export-Import Bank credits, in large part still unused.[6] Nevertheless, the Truman administration was coming under powerful pressure from elements in the country and in the Congress that charged it with not having done enough on behalf of the Chinese government and that seemed to want the United States to involve itself inextricably in what many of us saw as a hopeless cause.

In July 1947, on the recommendation of General Marshall, President Truman directed General Wedemeyer, known to be a firm friend of the nationalist government, to proceed to China on a fact-finding mission. While in China, in accordance with a suggestion by Chiang Kai-shek, Wedemeyer addressed an assemblage of high officials of the Chinese government. He declared that the government could not defeat the Communists by force, but only by winning the support of the people through political and economic reforms. Chiang was offended, and in effect rejected this prescription: in discussions with Wedemeyer he said that when the problem of the Communists had been solved—presumably by military means—he would be able to concentrate on political and economic reforms.[7] Shortly after Wedemeyer's departure, Chiang asserted in a speech to Kuomintang leaders that China would never again depend on the United States for assistance, and that, while remaining friendly with the United States, China would have to strengthen its relations with the Soviet Union.[8]

In his report to the president, General Wedemeyer at one point expressed the opinion that a U.S. policy conducted "without regard to the continued existence of an unpopular repressive government would render any aid ineffective." General Marshall would certainly have agreed. Marshall's year's effort in China would surely have taught him that Chiang, as he made explicit to Wedemeyer, was intent on dealing with the Communists first, and would leave the matter of reforms for later. Why, then, did he advise the president to send Wedemeyer on this mission? I was told at the time by Arthur Ringwalt, chief of the Division of Chinese Affairs and my immediate superior, that its purpose was to relieve the pressure for a deeper U.S. commitment, and thus to gain time.

Having completed his mission and submitted his report,

Wedemeyer was admonished by Marshall to scrupulously avoid discussing its contents with anyone. When a copy was supplied to us in the Division of Chinese Affairs, it was with a similar warning. In justifying his suppression of the report, Marshall subsequently described it as motivated by the belief that one of Wedemeyer's recommendations—that Manchuria, then being overrun by Chinese communist forces, should be placed under a five-power or U.N. trusteeship—would be resented by the Chinese as an attempt to alienate Chinese territory. In addition, I suspect, Marshall found another of Wedemeyer's recommendations even more objectionable. In an annex to his report, despite what he had said about the unsuitability of aid not accompanied by reforms, Wedemeyer recommended that U.S. military advice and supervision be extended in scope to include Chinese forces in the field.[9] He estimated that extending such assistance down to the regimental level would require about ten thousand commissioned and noncommissioned officers.[10] This would have been a long step toward full military intervention, and in discussing the matter with Walton W. Butterworth, director of the State Department's Office of Far Eastern Affairs, Marshall declared that if he were to intervene militarily, he would need half a million men just to start with. And how, he asked, would he ever be able to extricate them?[11] It will be appreciated that we in the Division of Chinese Affairs abided gladly, as well as scrupulously, by General Marshall's injunction not to disclose the contents of the Wedemeyer Report.

In March 1949 I was transferred to Manila, where I served for two years as chief of the U.S. Embassy's political section. It was the time of the rebellion of the Hukbong Mapagpalaya ng Bayan (HMB), successors of the wartime Hukbalahap guerrillas. The HMB was under the direction of the Philippine Communist Party, which was hoping to succeed through the strategy by which the Chinese Communists were defeating the Nationalists on the adjacent Asian mainland. It was my responsibility in Manila to learn all I could about the Huks, to follow both their operations and the efforts of the government to suppress them closely, and to prepare analytical reports on the rebellion for transmission to Washington. It also fell to my lot on occasion to recommend measures the United States might undertake, and one such occasion came just after a number of spectacularly successful Huk raids, conducted simultaneously on the 29 March 1950 anniversary of the founding of the Hukbalahap.

As was made evident in a report I drafted on behalf of the embassy at that time, the Philippine armed forces were in urgent need of better and stronger military leadership. Our report stated: "So long as the Constabulary seize foodstuffs without paying for them, become drunk and disorderly, extract information by inhumane methods, abuse women, shoot up country towns and mistreat the populace, just so long will they continue to lose the Philippines to the HMB." In that same message we recommended that the United States assign to Manila, in an advisory role, military personnel with knowledge of and experience with political subversion and guerrilla warfare such as the Philippine government was facing.[12]

Somewhat later Ambassador Myron M. Cowen invited a number of us, including Major General Jonathan W. Anderson, chief of the joint U.S. military advisory group, to accompany him on a trip aboard the embassy air attaché's plane. During our flight, General Anderson told me that President Elpidio Quirino was going to appoint a new secretary of national defense and had asked for his recommendations. Anderson then produced a list of a number of possible choices, which we discussed. It contained the name of Ramon Magsaysay, and because I knew him to have had wartime guerrilla experience, I said he was the one I would recommend—as did Ambassador Cowen. Magsaysay undoubtedly was the first choice of General Anderson, who knew him well in his capacity as chairman of the armed forces committee of the Philippine lower house. In any event, on 1 September 1950, President Quirino appointed Magsaysay secretary of national defense, and while I was one of those who took satisfaction in the appointment, I would never have imagined how successful he would prove to be. Nor, for that matter, did I know Colonel, later Major General, Edward G. Lansdale, sent to the Philippines in an advisory role such as I had envisaged, whose relationship with Magsaysay was to prove so fruitful.

Not long after Magsaysay assumed office, he is said to have

played an important role in the discovery in a downtown Manila office building of the headquarters of the Philippine Communist Party and in the arrest of a number of its leaders. A night raid on that headquarters yielded a great quantity of documents. The embassy was able to obtain photocopies of these, and their contents contributed greatly to our knowledge of both the Huks and the Philippine Communist Party.

In 1951—the same year, incidentally, in which the Huk rebellion was reaching and passing its peak—I had the good fortune to be chosen to spend a year as a student at the National War College, followed by a tour of duty at Stuttgart as consul general and land commissioner for Baden-Württemberg under the U.S. High Commission for Germany. Baden-Württemberg contained the headquarters of the U.S. Army, Europe, at Heidelberg, as well as those of the U.S. Eighth Army and its Fifth Corps, both in Stuttgart itself. The Fifth Corps was commanded by Lieutenant General James M. Gavin: already the author of *Airborne Warfare,* he was well read in the field of unconventional military operations and made available to me a number of works on the subject that might otherwise never have come to my attention.

In the autumn of 1959 I became a member of the State Department's Policy Planning Staff, soon thereafter redesignated the Policy Planning Council, and in the files left behind by a predecessor I found a voluminous study of irregular warfare in Colombia and an instructive report on what was called the Emergency in Malaya. This led me to begin working on what was intended to be a paper on the subject of wars of the kind through which the Chinese Communists had come to power, and that I had followed in the Philippines, but also based on the materials I had found in the files. However, I soon was assigned instead to other work on the grounds that guerrilla warfare was a military subject.

John F. Kennedy held the quite different view that guerrilla warfare, in which he had a lively interest, was political as well as military in nature, and after his inauguration in January 1961 all parts of the foreign affairs apparatus of the government were called upon to concern themselves with counterinsurgency. In the early 1960s President Sukarno seemed to be allying himself with the Communist Party of Indonesia; he talked much of a Djakarta–Phnom Penh–Peking–Pyongyang axis; and one was bound to surmise that he was being encouraged in Peking, where he was a welcome visitor, in his paramilitary attacks on Malaysia. And the Middle Eastern oil on which Japan was vitally dependent had to pass by tanker through the Strait of Malacca, flanked by Indonesia and Malaysia—a circumstance that suggested that the assumed collaboration between China and Indonesia represented a threat that was not limited to Malaysia. Moreover, communist China was giving political, economic, and military assistance to North Vietnam, contributing to the impression that it was thrusting outward. We could not then foresee that Sukarno would be overthrown in an anticommunist coup in the latter part of 1965, or that the Democratic Republic of Vietnam and the People's Republic of China would in 1979 fight a border war.

Against the background of the world view that then prevailed in Washington, and in the atmosphere of compulsive activism that characterized the new administration, I drafted a paper for the Policy Planning Council proposing that U.S. embassies in countries deemed vulnerable to communist insurgency be instructed to prepare appraisals of the situation in their host nations, including a statement of what each country's government needed to do for the purpose of improving its administration and attracting the support of its people and an estimate of its ability to take the requisite measures. The governments in question were to be encouraged to carry those measures out, with the United States standing ready to supply the difference between what needed to be done and what they could do for themselves. This had about it an element of accepting imperial responsibilities without having imperial authority, which troubled me at the time, though I was less dubious then than I have since become about the utility of interventions in the affairs of other lands. In any case, though my paper underwent much change at other hands, the approach I had suggested was incorporated in relevant National Security Action memorandums and led to the formulation by U.S. embassies in a number of countries of so-called Country Internal Defense Plans.[13]

It was not the intention, in my own mind at least, that U.S.

commitments to foreign governments should be open-ended, and it was particularly in the sphere of military involvement that I believed limits needed to be observed. Thus, on 11 May 1961, I prepared on behalf of the Policy Planning Council a memorandum commenting on a National Security Council paper and dissenting with some courses of action proposed to be taken by the United States with respect to the deteriorating situation in South Vietnam. In that memorandum, an expurgated copy of which has been released to me under the Freedom of Information Act, I wrote: "We are skeptical of the utility of employing US flag forces in a counter-guerrilla capacity in Vietnam. If the measures outlined in this plan prove insufficient, we doubt the situation will be remediable through the use of foreign troops." I realized, I added, that this ran counter to the expressed opinions of Lieutenant General Lionel C. McGarr, chief of the U.S. Military Mission in Saigon, who was being quoted as saying that he could clean up the Viet Cong in a few months with two or three regiments of the sort of troops he commanded in World War II.

In that same memorandum I suggested the desirability of better preparing the forces of the government of South Vietnam (GVN) for coordinated small-unit operations rather than accepting proposals, contained in an annex to the NSC paper, for the "prompt organization of two new GVN divisions" and for putting "the entire GVN army through a greatly intensified divisional training program," a program that would have better prepared South Vietnam to meet a conventional invasion, but not to conduct counterinsurgency operations.

I made points similar to those contained in that memorandum in a paper I prepared that same year, which was among the study materials adopted for use by the Counter Guerrilla Department of the Special Warfare School at Fort Bragg. However, I doubt that either memorandum had any effect on subsequent decisions. In any case, the army chief of staff professed to believe that any good soldier could handle guerrillas, and army Special Forces were never given more than a limited role in Vietnam.[14] The United States agreed, in response to a letter from President Diem, to underwrite the creation of the two new divisions.[15] The entire army of South Vietnam could not have been put through an intensified divisional training program in any case, given the problems it was having in coping with increasing numbers of Viet Cong guerrillas. And it was on the basis of his own judgment that the president resisted the early deployment of U.S. ground troops in Vietnam, a measure recommended by the Joint Chiefs of Staff as early as 10 May 1961.[16]

Late in 1961 Averell Harriman was appointed assistant secretary of state for far eastern affairs and chose me to serve under him as deputy assistant secretary. He had been entrusted by President Kennedy with responsibility for negotiations being conducted in Geneva intended to lead to the neutralization of Laos; in consequence there were periods when he was away from Washington; and when he was absent I served as acting assistant secretary. The president's policy on Laos had many opponents, and while Harriman was away I sometimes found myself fending off efforts by Secretary of State Dean Rusk to have me take steps that in my opinion would have tended to undermine it.

Here I should recall that both Chinese regimes, Mao Zedong's People's Republic of China, governing the mainland, and Chiang Kai-shek's Republic of China, occupying Taiwan and a number of smaller islands, were then—as they still are—within artillery range of each other at the point where the heavily fortified nationalist-held island of Quemoy faces the mainland port of Amoy. Because the United States was committed under a treaty of alliance concluded in 1955 to the defense of Taiwan, any attempt by either side to test the defenses of the other in the Quemoy-Amoy area would threaten to involve the United States—as, indeed, it had in 1958.

In the early months of 1962 it became evident that in consequence of the failure of Mao's economic policies, the people of China were suffering from widespread hunger. In this situation Chiang professed to believe that it would take little—perhaps only the landing of a division of nationalist troops—to trigger a mass uprising and enable him to return to power on the mainland. Meanwhile, his son, Chiang Ching-kuo, attempted through the CIA station chief in Taipei to gain the backing of the United States for this venture.

In June it became apparent that the Communists had begun an enormous troop buildup along the coast opposite Taiwan. Because the preparations did not include the gathering of the craft that would have been needed for an invasion of Quemoy, much less of Taiwan, it appeared that the buildup was defensive in nature, but the situation nevertheless seemed potentially explosive. At the juncture President Kennedy, Secretary of State Dean Rusk, and Secretary of Defense Robert McNamara were united in determination that force should not be used in the vicinity of the Taiwan Strait by either side. Near the end of June, Harriman prepared a message to be transmitted to the Chinese Communists, through ambassadorial contacts maintained with them at Warsaw, making it clear that any nationalist attempt to invade the mainland would have no U.S. support. The Communists recognized that a nationalist invasion not supported by the United States would be a suicidal venture and, despite further nationalist probes, the crisis soon passed.[17]

That same year Harriman took steps designed to discourage Chiang Kai-shek from resorting to further ventures of the same kind. He had Everett F. Drumright, who had by then served as ambassador in Taipei for four years, replaced by Admiral Alan G. Kirk. In China, as is well known, age carries with it the right to receive a certain deference; Admiral Kirk was of about the same age as Chiang Kai-shek, whereas Ambassador Drumright was decades younger. As a former ambassador to the Soviet Union, Kirk was an experienced diplomat. Most to the point of all, he had commanded the U.S. task forces for the invasions of Sicily and Normandy during World War II, and was in position to enlighten Chiang on what was required for conducting a major amphibious landing.

In the spring of 1963, Harriman was promoted to the post of undersecretary of state for political affairs. In discussing with me the question of who was to succeed him in the position he was relinquishing, Harriman paid me the compliment of saying that things had gone as well in his absences as when he was present. However, while I appreciated that expression of his confidence, I had no expectation of being offered the post. It was not only that I had undoubtedly irked Secretary Rusk during the periods in which I had been in charge of the Bureau of

Far Eastern Affairs. When on the Policy Planning Council, I had been informed that the secretary disapproved of my approach to China policy. I at no time recommended U.S. recognition of the Peking government, but I had concluded that the Chinese government on Taiwan could not be kept in the United Nations much longer by trying to keep the Peking government out. In any case, I was told that the secretary did not want me to testify on the subject of U.S. policy toward China before committees of the Congress, and I knew he would not accept a proposal for my promotion.

Harriman was succeeded by Assistant Secretary of State Roger Hilsman, with whom I had collaborated in his immediately prior position as the department's director of intelligence and research. Hilsman, under whom I served until the end of 1963, was a West Point graduate who had led Burmese guerrillas against the Japanese during World War II, and he brought this experience to bear on the problems of Southeast Asia in general and Vietnam in particular throughout his period in the Department of State.

On 22 November Hilsman was host at a luncheon held on the eighth floor of the State Department honoring Senator Raul S. Manglapus of the Philippines at which Undersecretary Harriman, Senator Frank Church, and others besides myself were among the guests. Halfway through the meal, Senator Church was called to the phone. He suddenly appeared stricken, and returned to give us the news that President Kennedy had been shot. Kennedy had to the last resisted the introduction of U.S. troops in Vietnam in combat roles, but with his death a chapter was closed.

I had by the end of 1963 served in the Department of State for five years and was glad to be sent to Hong Kong as consul general, a post I was to hold until the latter part of 1967. We did not have diplomatic relations with Peking at the time, and Hong Kong served as our principal listening post for mainland China. I became deeply preoccupied with its affairs in consequence of the active military and economic support it was giving North Vietnam and of the outbreak in China itself of the so-called Cultural Revolution. A short time after I left the department, William P. Bundy succeeded Hilsman as assistant secretary. Bundy made it his practice to solicit the views regarding Vietnam of all the chiefs of mission in his geographic area of responsibility, usually by telegram, but also at periodic chiefs-of-mission conferences. Bundy welcomed dissenting views, and I was often ready to oblige.

While I was in Hong Kong and after the Cultural Revolution had begun, the secret files of the Chinese Communist Party were in large part opened up to the rampaging Red Guards, the news sheets they set up operated free of censorship, and travel controls between mainland China and Hong Kong were loosened. In consequence, quantities of highly informative Red Guard newspapers reached Hong Kong. A substantial portion was translated by various organizations, including the press monitoring service of our own consulate general, and made available to the public. During that same period Chinese Communists, using methods of agitation and terrorism, tried unsuccessfully to take over Hong Kong from within.

At the end of my tour in Hong Kong, I was given a final assignment as diplomat-in-residence at the University of California in Berkeley, where I was attached to the Center for Chinese Studies. Among the materials in its library were copies of the translations from the Red Guard press made in Hong Kong, and this enabled me to begin writing my book *Mao's Way*, a study of the Chinese Revolution, which after its completion some years later was published by the University of California Press. In turn, work on that book led me to reconsider the Chinese revolution as a model Communists elsewhere—notably in Vietnam and in the Philippines—had sought to adapt to their own purposes.

Meanwhile I was coming to realize that while conclusions I had reached about wars of the third kind on the basis of my own observations were themselves communicable, my convictions concerning their general validity perhaps were not. This tended to negate their value in deciding questions of war and peace, not only for government officials but also for the populace, which needs to keep watch over the latter's performance.

The solution to this problem was suggested to me by an interchange between two eminent political scientists on the implications of the Vietnam conflict for future U.S. foreign policy. One of them, Samuel P. Huntington, declared: "It is conceivable that our policy-makers may best meet future crises and dilemmas if they simply blot out of their minds any recollection of this one." In support of this assertion, he made the points that the situational characteristics of our Vietnamese entanglements were in many respects unique, and that any lessons learned from it might be the wrong ones. In reply to these assertions, Hans Morgenthau, the other noted political scientist, observed that it was no new discovery that historical phenomena are unique in one sense, but that it also is obvious that they are in another sense typical.[18] The problem, then, is to identify those aspects of historical phenomena that are typical, and to draw from them the lessons they contain.

Accordingly, I decided to examine a convincingly large number of wars of the third kind, occurring in a variety of countries and in different historical periods. I would need to distinguish between the particularities of each such war and the respects in which it was typical, establish the strategic principles underlying these wars, and draw any other generalizations my study might reveal—a time-consuming task, but one I found rich in interest.

The chapters that follow set forth the results of this inquiry.

1 *Recurrence and Radicalization in Wars of the Third Kind*

Wars for independence may be defeated and rebellions may be suppressed, leaving the aims for which they were fought unattained. However, after a time, if the problems that gave rise to them are fundamental, defeated or suppressed struggles are likely to be resumed. Moreover, much as a second attack of a recurrent fever is likely to prove more virulent than the one that preceded it, a cause is likely to become radicalized by passing through a cycle of suppression and reemergence.

The first of the two wars of the third kind that Cubans fought against Spain arose out of frustrated demands for reform. In 1823 there had been a liberal upsurge in Spain and its colonial empire; by 1825 all the countries of continental Latin America had become independent, and in Cuba there were stirrings that led to the imposition of martial law. It was left in force for fifty years, and by the mid 1860s the need for change had become urgent. Following the abolition of slavery in the United States, the illegal African slave trade was finally being brought to an end, and progressive planters saw a need to shift to cultivation of the land by freeholders who might be encouraged to immigrate from Spain. This was but one item—though an important one—on an agenda of problems, and early in 1866 a

Cuban commission journeyed to Madrid, where a liberal government was prepared to consider them. That government fell just as the commission arrived, but the new colonies minister received its members, all their demands were discussed, and when they left in the spring of 1867, it was in the belief that action would follow. It did not, nor had the new Spanish government intended that it should. As that became apparent, the reformers gave up and revolutionaries took over.[1]

Those who rose in 1868 were for the most part the small sugar planters, coffee farmers, and cattle ranchers of eastern Cuba, including some who were too poor to afford slaves and others who were prepared for emancipation. The great plantations were, for the most part, situated toward the western end of the island, and their owners held aloof, fearing that a war against Spain would risk devastation and the loss of their slaves.[2] In Havana, also situated well to the west, the criollo population was not dominant, and many thousands of *peninsulares* joined bodies of loyalist militia, known collectively as the Volunteers, and fought on the side of their native land.[3] Indeed, in order to hold and protect the western end of the island, the Spanish created a great fortified ditch, thirty miles long, which ran from one side of the island to the other at its narrowest point.[4] Most of the fighting took place beyond this *trocha,* and there the war was fought with great cruelty. The orders to Spanish troops were to kill every male over the age of fifteen who was found away from his place of habitation and to burn any house that either was unoccupied or was not flying a white flag as signal of a desire for peace. The Volunteers, in their operations, did not customarily make such distinctions. Rather, they made it a practice to kill every living thing they encountered and to burn all the houses that they found.[5]

In 1877 Spain sent to Cuba General Martínez de Campos, a humane and honorable man, together with a reinforcement of twenty-five thousand men. After years of conflict, rebel morale was at a low ebb, and General Martínez combined a vigorous campaign with offers of land from the crown holdings to deserters and of amnesty to those who laid down their arms. This combination, together with the promise of reforms, proved irresistible, and in 1878 the last of the rebels surrendered.[6] In

1886 the slaves were freed, but most of the other promised reforms did not take place, and the cost of the war was added to the Cuban debt.[7]

Much as the way to World War II was paved by World War I, the insurrection of 1868–78 proved the forerunner of the Cuban war for independence that began in 1895. The earlier conflict had accomplished little except to instill the realization that war brings much suffering and misery. By 1895, however, that sense had faded and been replaced by a growing alienation from Spanish rule. Moreover, there no longer was the same sharp division between the two parts of the island that had been represented by the *trocha,* for following emancipation, the rich planters no longer needed the Spanish army to protect them from their slaves. The exiled leaders of the earlier war, believing the time to be ripe, had secretly returned to their homeland, begun raising guerrilla bands in the hill country of eastern Cuba, and assigned posts to the leaders of what was to become the national government of Cuba. Spanish troops took the field, and thus the issue was joined.[8]

The Spanish government again sent Martínez de Campos to Havana as commander in chief and captain-general. After assessing the situation in Cuba, Martínez concluded that suppression of the rebellion would require the application to the whole country of the ruthless measures used in eastern Cuba during the earlier war, including reconcentration of the population. In reporting this conclusion to the prime minister, he expressed the opinion that even if Spain were to win in the field and suppress the rebels, whether with reforms or without, it would within twelve years again have a war on its hands. Moreover, Martínez concluded, the misery and suffering a policy of ruthless suppression would entail would be terrible, and he believed himself to be lacking in the qualities required for carrying it through. "Reflect my dear friend," he wrote, "and if after discussion you approve the policy I have described, do not delay in recalling me."

General Valeriano Weyler y Nicolau, arriving in Havana early in 1896 as the successor to Martínez, asserted that he would restore order within thirty days. In trying to make good this pledge, he had some four hundred thousand people removed from rural districts to garrison towns, after which the surrounding plantations were devastated in order to deny food to the rebels. More than two years later, the rebellion still continued; thousands of reconcentrated civilians had died of starvation, exposure, and disease; and in the United States public sympathy for the rebels and revulsion against Weyler's methods had been transmuted into public pressure for intervention, bringing on the Spanish-American War.

The defeat of Spain by the United States, however, placed Cubans in the position of having to agree to the limitations upon their independence embodied in the Platt amendment to legislation adopted by the U.S. Congress. The United States was to be allowed to lease land for a naval base—subsequently established at Guantánamo—with no date set for the lease's termination, and was to have the right to intervene in Cuba for the purposes of preserving its independence and of maintaining stable government. When the Platt amendment was under consideration, Senator J. B. Foraker had argued that it would prove self-defeating insofar as maintaining stable government was concerned. Those suffering defeat in Cuban elections would be tempted to create disorders that might invite intervention, hoping thereby to turn the tables on their opponents. In this prediction he proved prescient, and the United States found itself intervening in Cuba in 1906, 1912, 1917, 1920, and—although this time without actually landing troops—again in 1933.[9]

The Cuba of 1933 might be described, without much exaggeration, as an economic colony of the United States. Upward of three-quarters of the arable land was owned by foreigners, most of them individual Americans or U.S. corporations. Cuban agriculture was almost entirely devoted to sugar, and roughly 75 percent of all sugar capital was American. Most of Cuba's sugar lands had by now been consolidated into vast estates, where workers lived in what might be called company towns. The season for cutting the cane, a hectic period, lasted about three months, and replanting needed to be done only at intervals of five to twenty-five years. Thus over half the year was *tiempo muerto* for the average worker, during which he was unemployed, inasmuch as he had no land of his own to till, was likely to be tied by debt to the plantation on which he worked and lived, and was in any case situated far from any alternative source of employment.[10] In his *Sugar and Society in the Caribbean,* the Cuban historian Ramiro Guerra y Sánchez described the sugar latifundium as an engulfing organism, a system operating outside the public law, consolidating thousands of small farms, destroying the independent farming class, and putting an end to national economic independence. A free people who relinquish their land to another, he warned, "have taken the path to economic servitude and social and political decay."[11]

American capital also had a large stake in Cuba's railways and controlled a majority of the public utilities. In these fields American capital had a lesser role in the lives of the people of Cuba. Nevertheless it is not irrelevant that the American-owned Cuban Electric Company, the largest of the public utilities by far, charged rates a reliable American commentator could only describe as "outrageous."[12]

The U.S. intervention of 1933 was occasioned by disorders that accompanied efforts to bring down President Gerardo Machado. He had been elected for a four-year term in 1925, but in 1928 had called a constitutional convention packed with his own men that, besides abolishing the vice presidency, granted him an additional six-year term, without reelection. Machado was guilty of colossal corruption and suspected of having arranged a number of killings that had taken place earlier in his administration. By 1933 his opponents were being openly hunted down by a *porra,* or gang of thugs, in the pay of one of his henchmen.[13] The principal opponents of Machado were students of the University of Havana, which he had closed down in 1930, often led by their professors or by other men no longer of student age, and a secret organization of middle-class composition, founded in 1931, called ABC.[14] Its stated objectives, besides the overthrow of Machado, included the elimination of the latifundia, restriction on the acquisition of land by U.S. corporations, the establishing of producers' cooperatives, and the nationalization of public services. The ABC, like the Communist Party, was organized on the basis of cells, but it was denounced by the Communists because it expected, through its use of antigovernment terrorism, to bring on intervention by the United States.[15]

The new administration of Franklin D. Roosevelt, troubled by Machado's breach of the Cuban constitution and the incessant murders taking place under his administration, sent the diplomat Sumner Welles as ambassador to Havana with the mission of mediating between Machado and the opposition. He arrived early in May 1933, and it took him only a few days to reach the wrong conclusions that Machado had the unquestioned loyalty of the army, that he accordingly would be able to maintain order, and that the need for a change did not exist.[16] Within three months Welles received word from an army captain, passed through the embassy's military attaché, that the younger officers were in favor of Machado's overthrow; learned from a guerrilla outbreak, bombings, and various other happenings that Machado was not succeeding in maintaining order; and found that Machado's reaction to pressure for constitutional reform and preparation for elections was to stall.[17]

While Machado stalled and Welles continued his efforts at mediation, there began an epidemic of strikes and work stoppages, some of them planned and others apparently spontaneous. It began with telegraph workers, who had a genuine grievance—their pay was in arrears. But it then spread to newspaper printers, the men who delivered milk and ice, the bartenders, the waiters, until it seemed that everything was shutting down. With people standing about and asking when the American troops were to land, a group of senior officers, anxious to stave off armed intervention, approached Machado with blunt word that they were unanimous in demanding that he resign. The night of 12–13 August Machado flew with five friends to Nassau. The abruptness of their departure was evidenced by the circumstance that the five arrived there still in their pajamas.[18]

Welles now appeared to have considerable latitude, for the representatives of the higher officers had told him they would accept any Cuban he chose to succeed Machado.[19] In 1921, already working in the Department of State on Cuban affairs, Welles had written a memorandum in which he listed the six most desirable characteristics of a Cuban president. First on his list was a thorough acquaintance with the desires of the U.S. government; last was amenability to any advice offered him by

the American legation.[20] Now Welles settled on the diplomat
Carlos Miguel Céspedes, son of one of the liberators of 1898,
but himself colorless and a man of little force. Céspedes, who
was American-born and had been educated in the United
States, formed his cabinet the day after Machado's flight. Like
him, his ministers were men of North American outlook, and
according to Welles there was not a man among them who was
not of high personal integrity.[21] However, Welles had placed
power in the hands of a man unused to wielding it and without
general backing, on a day of great disorder on which upward of
a thousand people were killed, some three hundred homes were
sacked, and mobs threatened the police with lynchings.[22]

Machado had fallen when the senior officers withdrew their
support, and Céspedes was brought down by enlisted men.
Machado had drawn on the army for appointees, as though it
were a second civil service, and had used it for running monop-
olies controlling the distribution of milk and meat, practices
that opened wide opportunities for graft and for favoritism. He
had also sometimes appealed over the heads of the officers to
the interest of the sergeants, and their discipline had thereby
been weakened.[23] Having been favored by Machado and strong
in his support, they now feared they would be subjected to a
purge if they did not move to forestall it. Thus it was that in the
early hours of 5 September a group of them staged a takeover
of the army. The most vigorous and resourceful member of the
group proved to be Sergeant Fulgencio Batista, who proceeded
to designate the noncommissioned officer in each company
who was to assume command and to go about haranguing
those who were inclined to hold back. A number of the army's
younger commissioned officers wanted to take vigorous action
at once, but the senior commanders were slow in taking the
revolt seriously and never succeeded in regaining command.[24]
Céspedes was away, and the members of his cabinet, upon
hearing of the revolt, feared an attack and dispersed.

Before showing their hand, the sergeants had obtained assurances of civilian support, and on the morning of the revolt
the representatives of various organizations that had been left
out when Céspedes was forming his government joined Batista
and his associates at the military establishment known as Cam-

pamento Colombia. They proposed to take over the government, and elected a leadership group of five, soon known as the Pentarquía, composed of an honest banker, two lawyers, a newspaper publisher, and a doctor of medicine. The doctor of medicine was Professor Ramón Grau San Martín, recently returned from exile and little known to the populace at large, but a hero to the students as the only faculty member of his university who had voted against giving an honorary degree to Machado. Already there was discussion of the allocation of cabinet posts, and Batista was offered the portfolio of minister of defense, but declined, preferring to remain in command of the army and—though he did not say so—to retain his options.[25]

Early in the afternoon of the same day, Céspedes handed over the occupancy of the National Palace to Grau San Martín and the other members of the Pentarquía, who now regarded themselves as the government and were so regarded by others. However, on 7 and 9 September noncommissioned officers approached Céspedes in the name of Batista, offering to support Céspedes as president provided he would confirm Batista as head of the army. Céspedes each time refused, and on 10 September he took asylum in the Brazilian Embassy. Meanwhile the Pentarquía, despite grave misgivings, but with no alternative, had confirmed Batista as army chief of staff, and Grau San Martín had by common consent taken over the post of president.[26]

Sumner Welles, no doubt resentful of those who had undone his handiwork, was unwilling to accept a government headed by Grau San Martín, a university professor who was always surrounded by radical students carrying machine guns. He also refused to take Batista's pivotal position into account in seeking an alternative solution, and relations between them deteriorated to the point where the two no longer were on speaking terms.[27] If Cuba were to be stabilized under the government of Grau San Martín, or perhaps any government whatsoever, it needed the official recognition of the United States, and while Welles was ambassador, it would not be accorded contrary to his recommendations. Grau recognized that this was so, and as early as 17 September he offered to resign. This opened the way for

Welles to try to assemble a coalition of other elements under an acceptable leader, but in vain.[28] The consequence was a stalemate that might have been broken by U.S. military intervention, but Welles had three times asked for such intervention early in September and had thrice been refused.[29] On 13 December, seeing no way out, Welles abandoned his mission and departed for Washington, to be succeeded by Jefferson Caffery.[30]

Three weeks after his arrival in Havana, Ambassador Caffery submitted a report to the Department of State saying that he agreed with his predecessor as to the inefficiency and ineptitude of the Grau San Martín government, and its unpopularity "with all the better classes of the country." It was supported, he said, only by the army and the ignorant masses (though in a subsequent telegram he admitted "that, in numbers, the ignorant masses of Cuba reach a very high figure"). Moreover, there was little time to spare, for elections to a constituent assembly were to be held in April. Caffery thought that they would be won by Grau's followers, and it would then be difficult for the United States to continue to deny him recognition.[31]

In essence, Caffery decided to convey the message that he, like Welles, disapproved of the Grau San Martín regime; to suspend the efforts at coalition building in which Welles had been engaged; and to give his unreserved support to Batista, whom he was soon joining for morning horseback rides and to attend cock fights.[32] As Caffery undoubtedly knew, the Communist Party of Cuba had condemned Grau's government, but Caffery in his first official contact with one of its ministers complained about its "communistic tendencies," citing as evidence a new Workmen's Compensation Law and the "confiscatory legislation" represented by a measure requiring the Cuban Electric Company to reduce its rates by 45 percent. In January 1934, during a dinner at which Caffery, Grau, and Batista were guests, Grau offered to broaden the base of his government through the inclusion of opposition elements, whereupon Caffery revealed his determination to avoid further coalition building by simply refusing to discuss the offer. Batista then asked what the U.S. conditions for recognition were, but Caffery turned the question aside, saying that the government of Cuba was a matter for Cubans to decide. On receiving this assurance from Caffery, Batista looked at Grau and said: "You will have to go."[33]

A few days later Caffery was informed by Batista that he had decided to name for the presidency the well-regarded politician Carlos Mendieta, who had been Machado's opponent for the presidency in 1924, and at Caffery's recommendation, U.S. recognition was promptly accorded.[34] Later that same year the United States negotiated a new accord with Cuba, terminating the provision embodied in a treaty of 1903 that gave the United States the right to intervene in Cuba's internal affairs. At the same time Cuba confirmed the lease of the naval base at Guantánamo, still with no mention of a termination date.[35]

It took more than a year for violence in Cuba to die down and for the new government to consolidate its hold on the country, but for the next quarter century Cuban politics were dominated, whether through puppet presidents or directly, by Fulgencio Batista.[36] He and his supporters enriched themselves, much as Machado and his henchmen had done. Meanwhile, Cuba's natural resources, its public utilities, and its industries remained largely in the hands of foreigners, most of them Americans, and nothing was done about initiating badly needed land reform.[37] In response to the guerrilla war waged against him by Fidel Castro and his supporters, beginning in 1956, Batista had recourse to torture and executions, much as Machado had hired gangs of killers to track down members of the ABC and other opponents.[38] In doing so, Batista made additional enemies: indeed, according to a memorandum of 23 December 1958 sent President Eisenhower by acting Secretary of State Christian Herter, Batista had managed to alienate the great majority of the Cuban people. "The Department has concluded," Herter wrote, "that any solution in Cuba requires that Batista must relinquish power. . . . He probably should also leave the country."[39] Batista seems to have been reaching the same conclusion: at any rate, on New Year's Eve he and a planeload of relatives suddenly departed for the Dominican Republic, much as Machado and several friends had suddenly flown off to Nassau one night in 1933.

Collective memory north of the Rio Grande of U.S. involvement in the internal affairs of Central American countries may be short, but that of their peoples is long. U.S. histories afford scant space to William Walker, the North American leader of a force of filibusters who made himself president of Nicaragua and received diplomatic recognition from the United States in the days of President Franklin Pierce. But the anniversary of the day on which Walker was defeated by a regional army is celebrated each year throughout Central America.[40] More recently, in 1909, the United States began to use U.S. marines to install and keep in office Nicaraguan presidents favorably disposed toward U.S. interests. It was not until the mid 1920s that a Nicaraguan leader emerged whose nationalism made him militant and intractable.

In 1924 the United States supervised the most nearly honest election conducted so far in Nicaragua. In it, the presidency had been won by Carlos Solórzano, a Conservative, and the vice presidency by Juan B. Sacasa, a Liberal, after which the marines were withdrawn. Shortly thereafter, Emiliano Chamorro, a former president and the chief of the Conservative Party, forced Solórzano out, purged the legislature, and had it return him to the presidency. In no position to mount a successful challenge to the boss of his own party, Solórzano could only withdraw. Sacasa fled to the United States, where he attempted in vain to gain recognition as Nicaragua's rightful president, and then went to Mexico, where President Plutarco Elías Calles proved ready to grant him assistance. Inside Nicaragua, Sacasa was backed by General José María Moncada, and with the help of arms and ammunition supplied by Mexico, Moncada's forces soon were gaining the upper hand.[41]

The Mexican government had but recently seized American-owned lands, and it was threatening to expropriate the interests of foreign oil companies. In the United States the assistance Mexico was giving Sacasa was seen as a challenge to the primacy of the United States in Central America. With the help of the Mexican labor movement, Secretary of State Frank B. Kellogg asserted, Soviet Bolshevism was taking over the whole region. In dealing with this peril the Coolidge administration sent Colonel Henry L. Stimson to Nicaragua, arranging for him to arrive aboard the cruiser USS *Trenton,* and to be backed by a large contingent of marines.[42] Stimson worked out an agreement in the spring of 1927 under which the troops of both sides were to lay down their arms; in 1928 new elections were to be held; and a supposedly apolitical National Guard was to be organized, initially to be commanded by American officers. The Conservatives, militarily on the defensive, readily agreed, but Moncada held out until Stimson made it clear that the alternative was to find his forces pitted against the U.S. marines.[43]

Among Moncada's generals there were two who now took divergent roads: Anastacio Somoza García and Augusto César Sandino. Through schooling and employment in the United States, Somoza had gained a fluent command of American English, and Stimson, who spoke no Spanish, found him invaluable as an interpreter. Indeed, Somoza's relationship with Stimson and other Americans was to lead in 1932 to his appointment as the first Nicaraguan chief director of the National Guard. Sandino, having taken up arms in support of Sacasa, refused to lay them down. Instead, after fighting one bloody battle against the marines, he withdrew into the rugged mountains along the Honduran-Nicaraguan border.[44]

In the 1928 elections, held as had been agreed under U.S. supervision, General Moncada won the presidency. This event was overshadowed, however, by the reemergence of Sandino as leader of a guerrilla resistance that lasted until 1933, a resistance one historian has described as "a remarkable preview of the sixties in Vietnam."[45] Sandino had nothing against the American people, he declared, but would fight until the last U.S. troops had left Nicaraguan soil. The Coolidge administration sent in more marines, but neither they nor the American-officered National Guard were able to run Sandino to ground. In the United States the casualties suffered by the marines in Nicaragua made the intervention unpopular, and after the coming in 1929 of the Great Depression, it came to be seen as an unwarranted expense. American coffee planters in Nicaragua also came to see the intervention as a calamity. One of them wrote to Secretary of State Stimson: "Today we are hated and despised. This feeling has been created by employing American marines to hunt down and kill Nicaraguans in their own country."[46]

In 1932, now secretary of state in the cabinet of President Hoover, Stimson directed that Nicaragua should again hold elections. In these elections, Sacasa—the same Juan B. Sacasa

whose bid for the presidency had raised for Stimson's immediate predecessor the specter of a Bolshevik takeover—was elected to succeed Moncada as president. The U.S. government
was apparently unperturbed by his victory, for the withdrawal
of the marines went forward without a hitch. On 1 January
1933, President Sacasa was sworn into office, and that same day
the marines turned over command of the National Guard to
Somoza. The following day, the last of the marines left, finally
bringing the American occupation to an end.[47]

With the achievement of the purposes for which he had
taken up arms—Sacasa's claim to the presidency and the withdrawal of American troops—Sandino returned to Managua,
and there the two men readily reached an agreement. Sandino
was to be given control of a large region of virgin lands in
northern Nicaragua, where he proposed to set up an agricultural cooperative. His troops were to be demobilized by stages
until only a personal guard of one hundred men remained, and
after a year its future was to be reviewed. On 22 February 1933
about one thousand of his men were demobilized, in the presence of a large National Guard delegation, but they turned in
fewer than four hundred weapons, mostly rifles of various
makes, and National Guard officers suspected them of holding
back weapons.[48] After all, the two forces had been fighting for
upward of four years, and there was no trust between them.
Indeed, clashes between them continued throughout 1933, and
Sandino, in what Somoza must have seen as a challenge, asserted that the National Guard was unconstitutional and called
for it to be disbanded.[49]

It was the observation of Willard L. Beaulac, who served in
Managua as second secretary of the American legation from
1929 to 1933, that President Sacasa both knew Somoza well—
they were, in fact, related by marriage—and had never trusted
him. No doubt aware of that lack of trust, Sandino is said to
have offered the protection of his own forces to Sacasa. Such,
then, was the set of relationships in February 1934 when the
future of Sandino's remaining forces was to be reviewed and he
once again came to Managua. On the evening of 21 February,
leaving the presidential palace after a pleasant dinner as guests
of Sacasa's, Sandino and two of his officers were stopped by

men acting on Somoza's orders, taken to the airfield, and shot in the glare of the headlights of a truck.[50]

It having become apparent that Somoza was maneuvering to take the presidency from Sacasa, some of the latter's supporters laid plans to attack Somoza before it was too late.[51] However, they were dissuaded by the American minister, Arthur Bliss Lane, who was motivated by concern for Nicaragua's political stability, and the plans were dropped.[52] In 1936 President Sacasa and two ex-presidents, Oscar Díaz and Emiliano Chamorro, both of whom had supported the United States in the past, sent a pathetic letter to Secretary of State Hull recalling their fears that the National Guard the United States had created would eventually become a threat, despite assurances that it would be apolitical, and asking for U.S. protection against it. Hull sent them a cold response, saying that any special relationship between the United States and Nicaragua had ended when the marines withdrew.[53] In June 1936 Somoza forced Sacasa to resign, and later that same year he had himself elected president.[54]

Nicaragua was ruled during the next forty-three years by Anastacio Somoza García himself, informally known as Tacho, Luis Somoza Debayle, the elder of two sons, and his brother Anastacio Somoza Debayle, called Tachito. Both sons were educated in the United States. Luis attended Louisiana State University, while Tachito went to West Point, where he was a member of the class of 1946. Upon returning to Nicaragua Tachito was given the command of the National Guard as a graduation present. "Nicaragua," the elder Somoza declared, "es mi finca"—is my plantation—and he and his sons went far toward making it so. During the period of their rule, they acquired a quarter of the country's cultivated land. Much of it was converted to the raising of export crops, principally cotton and coffee. This involved driving hundreds of thousands of peasants from the land, and this conversion reduced the availability of the staple corn and beans on which the peasantry and the urban poor depended.[55] The Somozas also came to own 130 businesses and industries and great quantities of rental property. Together with officers of the National Guard, they monopolized gambling and prostitution. The economy grew, but public education and social services remained underdeveloped. Most of the urban and rural poor lived on the verge of starvation, with half the children dying by the age of five, most of them of gastrointestinal diseases.[56] It should be added that the regime was guilty of the use of torture against its opponents, most notably in its final years, during which the opposition grew.[57]

In Washington these matters did not go entirely unnoticed, but the Somozas made the manipulation of American officialdom an art, which they practiced to great effect. The elder Somoza during the 1930s had expressed admiration for Hitler and Mussolini and copied them by creating a fascist-style paramilitary force known as the Blue Shirts, but when World War II broke out, he declared Nicaragua on the side of the allies, leading President Franklin D. Roosevelt to remark: "Somoza may be a son-of-a-bitch, but he's our son-of-a-bitch."[58] Indeed, in 1939 Roosevelt received him warmly in Washington, and while there Somoza was invited to address a joint session of the Congress. In various international organizations, the United States could always count on the support of Somoza's government, and when he was shot in 1956—his assailant was an idealistic poet—President Eisenhower sent his personal physician in a vain attempt to save the dictator's life.[59] The elder son, Luis, who succeeded him, died of a heart attack in 1963. He was succeeded in turn by his brother Anastacio Somoza Debayle, whom President Nixon received at the White House during his first term. Somoza allegedly sent his mother to Washington during Nixon's reelection campaign with a contribution of $1 million in her handbag. On more than one occasion, too, the Somozas helped support military intervention by the United States in other countries of the region.[60]

Nicaragua had a military relationship with the United States that undoubtedly was the closest in the hemisphere. The Somozas were able to have all their officers spend a year at the U.S. School of the Americas in the Canal Zone, where they received counterinsurgency training in greater numbers than the officers of any other country. By 1967, with the rise of the Sandinista insurgency, there were twenty-five U.S. military advisers in Nicaragua, and up to the year of its fall, the Somoza regime was the recipient of generous amounts of U.S. military and economic assistance.[61] The successful cultivation of successive administrations in Washington, inducing as it did a confidence in the availability of U.S. backing, led the regime to underestimate the importance not only of having the support of its own people, but also of maintaining amicable relations with Nicaragua's neighbors. Costa Rica, in particular, several times accused Nicaragua of sponsoring right-wing invasions, and on one occasion it required the intervention of the Organization of American States to restore quiet along their common border.[62]

In 1961 three Nicaraguans—Carlos Fonseca, Tomás Borge, and Silvio Mayorga—believing that the Somoza regime could not be replaced by peaceful means and encouraged by the success of Castro and his supporters in overthrowing Batista in Cuba, founded the Frente Sandinista de Liberación Nacional (FSLN). However, they were separated from Sandino, whose name they were borrowing, not only by time, but by an ideological gulf as well. Sandino had had as secretary the Salvadoran Communist Agustín Farabundo Martí. But Sandino and the Communists of that earlier period did not get along, and Farabundo Martí, once he became convinced he could not convert Sandino to Marxism, abandoned his entourage. Later, Farabundo Martí wrote of Sandino: "His banner was only that of National independence . . . not social revolution."[63] However, unlike Sandino, all three of the founders of the FSLN were Marxist in their orientation.[64]

During the rule of Luis Somoza Debayle the FSLN leaders made their first attempt to establish a guerrilla base on Nicaraguan soil. In the latter part of 1962, after eighteen months of training at a jungle camp in Honduras, they and a few supporters tried to gain a foothold in territory of the Miskito Indians in which Sandino had once had a base. However, they blundered into a strong National Guard patrol, which killed some of them and scattered the rest. In December 1966 they tried again, this time centering their operations around Pancasan, a peak to the north of Lake Nicaragua, but abandoned the effort in the summer of 1967 after Silvio Mayorga and most of the others had been killed.[65] The Sandinistas also attempted to create a proletarian base by infiltrating existing unions and organizing new ones, but this effort suffered a setback in 1969 when the principal Sandinista leader engaged in it was among those killed in a shootout with National Guards. Indeed, a decade or so after the founding of the FSLN, it had no more than a score of men in the mountains undergoing guerrilla training and a handful of members in the cities. The compartmentalization the organization practiced kept this from being known to lower-ranking members, but the leaders knew how badly the Sandinistas needed allies.[66]

The FSLN did not gain those allies until after Luis had died and Nicaragua was under the misrule of Tachito. In December 1972 a localized but powerful earthquake destroyed the center of Managua, killing thousands of people and wiping out many businesses. It also revealed the basic weakness of the Somoza regime, for the discipline of the National Guard collapsed, with soldiers deserting to find their families or to engage in looting. The United States flew in troops from the Canal Zone to maintain order, and American and other foreign aid was rushed in, but medicines and food were taken by National Guard officers, sometimes at gunpoint, and some relief supplies were appropriated by civilian politicians. About half the $32 million supplied by the United States for reconstruction was never accounted for, and none of the money was used for the rebuilding of downtown Managua, or even for clearing away the rubble. The Somoza family and its associates held large parcels of land on the city's periphery, where they built new housing and shops. They thus profited from the disaster, but at the cost of pushing many families of the business and professional elite from dissatisfaction with the regime to active opposition.[67]

With presidential elections scheduled for 1974, Somoza had opposition parties declared illegal. When the leading newspaper *La Prensa* urged a boycott of the elections and printed stories of post-earthquake corruption, Somoza had its editor, Pedro Joaquín Chamorro, arrested and tried in the courts. In a pastoral letter, the Nicaraguan bishops condemned Somoza's attempts to force people to vote in the election, in which nothing was being left to chance, and after the election, they refused to attend the ceremonies marking the inauguration.[68]

At this time the general impression in Nicaragua was that the FSLN was either dead or dying, but on 27 December 1974 an event occurred that radically changed this perception. That evening a Sandinista band of ten men and three women invaded the home of a wealthy Managua businessman who was entertaining guests at dinner and took a number of them hostage, including a brother-in-law of Somoza's, the foreign minister, and a number of diplomats. The Sandinistas held them until Somoza had agreed to their terms: payment of a large ransom, the release of fourteen political prisoners, publication of a Sandinista communique, and arrangements under which the Sandinistas and the released prisoners would be safely flown out of the country. The happening captured widespread public attention, and crowds gathered to cheer the Sandinistas as they passed through the streets en route to the airport.[69]

The 27 December raid widened divisions within the FSLN, which contained three factions: the "proletarians," who advocated urban warfare, and who held that the raid reflected an unwillingness to devote the effort, however long it took, required for building proletarian consciousness; the advocates of the Maoist course of waging a protracted guerrilla war based on the peasantry; and the *terceristas,* advocates of a third way, some of whom had conducted the 27 December raid, who believed in reaching out to non-Marxists in the hope of producing a quick victory through a mass insurrection.[70] Carlos Fonseca, the most important of the three founders of the FSLN, cast his lot with the advocates of protracted guerrilla warfare and joined the members of that faction, who were based in the northern mountains. They became the targets of a two-year counter-insurgency campaign that Somoza launched in the wake of the 27 December raid, and on 8 November 1976 Fonseca was killed by National Guards. They took his head to Somoza, who concluded that they had eliminated the threat to his regime.[71]

The setbacks helped open the way for concentration on the strategy advocated by the *terceristas.* The implementation of *tercerista* plans owed much to the circumstance that the Somozas had earned the enmity of Costa Rica, Nicaragua's neighbor to the south, which permitted the formation, arming, and training on its soil of a Sandinista invasion force. Beginning in the autumn of 1977, this force began a series of incursions that helped light the fires of insurrection within Nicaragua itself.[72]

The *tercerista* strategy of building an alliance with the bourgeoisie received an enormous assist on the morning of 10 January 1978, when three men gunned down and mortally wounded Pedro Joaquín Chamorro, editor of *La Prensa*. His paper had been doing critical investigative reporting on a firm owned by Somoza that bought the blood of Nicaraguans and sold the plasma in the United States, but the reasons for Chamorro's assassination undoubtedly ran much deeper. A long-time opponent of the Somozas, Chamorro had been engaged in an effort to rebuild the Conservative Party as a vehicle of the opposition. On both his father's and his mother's sides, his forebears had been leaders of that party, and several of them had become president. Accordingly, the killing brought home to members of the bourgeoisie, more tellingly than anything had yet done, the nature of Somocista rule. Class status and the peaceful nature of the opposition in which he had been engaged had not protected Chamorro, and what had happened to him could happen to any one of them. The unwritten rules by which the game of politics had always been played in Nicaragua, which required a certain toleration within the circle of old families, had been broken, and the feeling ran among them that Somoza would have to go.[73]

When the body of Chamorro was taken home from the hospital to which it had been taken after the shooting, tens of thousands of people followed it. Two days later about ten thousand people took part in the funeral procession, while much larger numbers roamed the streets and engaged in violence. In the days that followed, an organization called the Superior Council of Private Initiative—an umbrella organization for chambers of commerce and industry—conducted a general strike that lasted for three weeks, and an ad hoc group of forty businessmen and professional leaders secretly joined the *tercerista* faction of the FSLN.[74]

On 21 February, a crowd of people in an Indian community some twenty miles from Managua, leaving a mass commemorating the forty days since the killing of Chamorro, was fired on by men of the National Guard. This provoked a rebellion in which fighting was heavy for a few days and continued sporadically thereafter.[75] At the end of February, unrest spread to other places, and there were clashes between youths and the

National Guard in such main centers as Managua and León. In order to exploit this situation, the Sandinistas created a body of forty men, who dispersed in main population centers, where they worked mainly among the urban poor.[76]

On 22 August 1978, the Nicaraguan congress, with a cousin of Somoza's presiding, was holding a session in the National Palace, and that morning over 1,500 people were in the building on one mission or another, when twenty-five *terceristas* wearing National Guard uniforms burst into the legislative chamber and took the members of congress hostage. What followed was a replay of the 27 December 1974 affair, but on a more impressive scale. Edén Pastora Gómez, the *tercerista* leader, negotiating through Archbishop Obando y Bravo over a period of forty-eight hours, obtained the release of sixty political prisoners, including Tomás Borge, in detention and undergoing torture for over a year, the payment of a large ransom, the publication of Sandinista communiques, and safe passage through cheering crowds to the airport for flights in planes provided by the governments of Venezuela and Panama.[77]

The palace raid inspired an apparently unplanned uprising by local youths in the city of Matagalpa, center of a coffee-growing region northwest of Managua, and it took the National Guard five days to retake the place. Shortly thereafter some Sandinistas launched hit-and-run attacks on National Guard posts around Managua and in other cities, and in some cases local people joined in and continued fighting after the Sandinistas had slipped away. In Estelí, where the fighting was most severe, the National Guards resorted to air attacks as part of their effort to subdue the uprising.[78]

As it became clear that the Somoza regime was nearing its end, the issue of what was to succeed it became an issue of increasing concern. In December it was announced over Cuba Radio that leaders of the three factions of the Sandinista Front had agreed to merge their forces and that Tomás Borge, now the surviving cofounder of the FSLN, was serving as coordinator of the unified leadership.[79] Meanwhile the efforts to rebuild the Conservative Party, which had been interrupted by the assassination of Chamorro, had yet to be resumed.[80] In the spring of 1979, when a 1,500-man Sandinista force began to invade Nicaragua from Costa Rica, it was under the command of Edén Pastora, who had led the palace raid. He had been fighting the Somozas on and off for almost twenty years,[81] but he was not a Marxist, and when a nine-man FSLN National Directorate was formed in Havana in March, he was not among those named to its membership.[82] Accordingly, when Somoza fled the country on 17 July, in the face of invasion from without and uprising within, it was men who had been divided over tactics and strategy, but not over ideology, who were organizationally prepared to take power.

From 1931 until 1944 Guatemala was ruled by General Jorge Ubico, most recent in a succession of military dictators who governed in the interests of a small landed aristocracy. However, during World War II a nascent Guatemalan middle class was influenced by President Franklin D. Roosevelt's assertion that all humanity was entitled to freedom of speech and religion and freedom from want and from fear. It was also impressed by the example of reforms carried out in Mexico under President Lázaro Cárdenas, who nationalized the country's oil resources, supported its labor movement, and gave new impetus to land reform. In 1944—beginning with school teachers striking for higher pay—people of nearly every walk of life staged demonstrations against Ubico's rule. At first he responded by declaring a state of siege and having his cavalry ride down demonstrating citizens. But after being presented with a petition expressing solidarity with the demonstrators signed by over three hundred prominent people, some of them his personal friends, Ubico resigned in a state of shock, turning over his office to a General Federico Ponce. The latter raised the pay of teachers and made a few cosmetic changes, but he turned people against him by intensified political repression, and in October 1944 two young officers led a coup in which he was overthrown.[83]

The young officers, joined by a prominent businessman, formed a governing junta. With the help of the Guatemalan Bar Association, they drew up a modern constitution, and in December 1944 they held elections. The favorite in these elections was Dr. Juan José Arévalo Bermejo, a professor of philosophy who now returned to Guatemala after fourteen years of exile. Arévalo's political heroes were Simón Bolívar, Abraham Lincoln, and Franklin D. Roosevelt. To many, he had himself become a political hero during his years of exile as a symbol of opposition to tyranny. Arévalo won 85 percent of the vote, and on 15 March 1945 he assumed office as the first popularly elected president of Guatemala.[84]

During Arévalo's presidency, with the Wagner Act as a model, a new labor code was enacted and a labor movement sprang into existence. The right to strike was not extended to agricultural workers, though peasants were encouraged to form purchasing and marketing cooperatives. More important in a country where 2 percent of the landowners held about three-quarters of the land, in 1949 a Law of Forced Rental was enacted that allowed peasants owning less than a hectare (2.47 acres) to petition for the right to rent unused land from the owners of nearby plantations. However, these and other reforms were only partially implemented during Arévalo's term in office, a turbulent period during which there were numerous coup attempts. In 1950 Jacobo Arbenz Guzmán, one of the leaders of the 1944 coup, was elected president; he assumed office in March 1951, and under him the reforms were pushed forward.[85]

As Arbenz was assuming office, the International Bank for Reconstruction and Development published a report written by Eugene Black, its president, which dealt with the glaring inequities of Guatemalan life and the urgent need for change. It called, among other things, for wages that took price levels into account; a tax on capital gains; regulation of foreign businesses; the establishment of a national power authority; and public spending on transportation, communications, and warehousing. In keeping with these recommendations, Arbenz began the construction of a publicly owned port on the Atlantic coast, a highway leading to it, and a government hydroelectric plant, measures that approached the problem of foreign domination of the economy by introducing competition rather than through nationalization.[86] In addition, however, the Arbenz administration adopted and began to implement legislation that empowered it to expropriate uncultivated portions of large estates, repaying the owners with interest-bearing government bonds based on the declared tax value of the land.[87]

In concluding his report for the International Bank for Reconstruction and Development, Eugene Black warned foreign companies against taking direct or indirect action against the government of Guatemala. Instead, he urged, they should "accept, perhaps less reservedly than they had thus far done, the need to adjust their legal status and their operations to changed conditions."[88]

The United Fruit Company, unfriendly to the direction taken by the government of Guatemala under Arévalo, found itself violently opposed to important measures put into effect under Arbenz. It owned 42 percent of Guatemala's land, but according to the later admission of one of the company's officials, it had only 139,000 of its 3 million acres planted to bananas in 1953, when the government began to expropriate land under its agrarian reform law. The company explained the practice of holding land in excess of its current needs as enabling it to shift cultivation to uninfected land when there were outbreaks of plant blight, but according to the later admission of one of its executives, it was also motivated by the wish to assure that competitors would not be able to use the land.[89] The United Fruit Company controlled Puerto Barrios, Guatemala's only port on the Atlantic, as well as the International Railways of Central America, which charged the highest freight rates in the world, and the government's port and highways project threatened to affect their profitability. The company also owned Empresa Eléctrica, which earned a return of over 100 percent, and this was threatened by the hydroelectric project.[90] Moreover, as the biggest employer in Guatemala, it could not expect to avoid the operation of labor laws ending the era in which it was able to prevent unionization, pay low wages, impose a seven-day work week, and refuse to allocate to its plantation workers small parcels of land that they could cultivate as private plots.[91]

There is dispute as to the amount of United Fruit Company land the government of Guatemala expropriated, with the totals ranging from 178,000 to 387,000 acres, but the protest made following the first expropriation was lodged not by the

United Fruit Company but by the Department of State.[92] The government of Guatemala had offered the company $627,572, or $2.99 an acre for land it had obtained twenty years earlier for slightly less than half that amount. Declaring that the amount offered bore "not the slightest resemblance to just evaluation," however, the note from the Department of State demanded that $75 an acre be paid for it.[93] Throughout the period that followed, Guatemalan officials were in negotiation with the Department of State for a resolution of the dispute. Meanwhile agrarian reform continued, and by 1954 it had enabled one hundred thousand peasant families to receive land, bank credits, and technical assistance. This enabled them to raise not only food for their own use and for sale on local markets, but crops for export as well, with the consequence that exports rose and the country attained a favorable balance of payments. The agrarian reform law also was engaging peasants in political affairs for the first time, for the reform was being run not from Guatemala City but by members of peasant unions at the local and provincial levels.[94]

While agrarian reform was going ahead the United Fruit Company was working quietly at the task of inducing the United States to take more drastic action on its behalf. One of its early steps was to utilize Edward Bernays, described as "the father of public relations," and a man who enjoyed personal acquaintance with the key people in American publishing and broadcasting circles, for the purpose of giving it the right image. As early as 1950, which is to say while Arévalo was still in the presidency, Bernays had expressed to company officials the thought that Guatemala "might respond to pitiless publicity in this country," and after Arbenz had assumed office Bernays undertook the task of subjecting Arbenz and his administration to the kind of publicity he had suggested.[95] In addition, the company engaged John Clements Associates to produce a long report on supposed Soviet intrusion in Guatemala, which it published anonymously and distributed anonymously to eight hundred "decision-makers." The same public relations firm also prepared a follow-up report arguing that Guatemala was ruled by Communists bent on conquering Central America and seizing the Panama Canal.[96]

Actually, in his inaugural speech Arbenz had stated that his government proposed to strengthen private initiative and to convert Guatemala from a backward country with a feudal economy into a modern capitalist state.[97] No Communists were ever admitted to cabinet-level government posts or to the army command. The agrarian reform, the most important program carried out by Arbenz's government, was never allowed to fall under communist control. However, there were four communist deputies in Arbenz's ruling coalition of fifty-one members, a number of Communists held posts at the working levels, urban unions had communist leaders, and Arbenz found Communists useful in carrying out his internal programs. In the United Nations his government supported Washington on major issues, including ones requiring it to take sides in the Cold War. Considering this picture as a whole, the reader may judge whether Guatemala had indeed fallen under communist control.[98]

However, in the Eisenhower administration there was an atmosphere sympathetic to the cause of the United Fruit Company. The president's personal secretary was the wife of Edmund S. Whitman, its director of advertising and publicity. Secretary of State John Foster Dulles had been a member of the law firm of Sullivan and Cromwell, which had drawn up the contract under which United Fruit had in 1936 acquired its Tiquisate plantation from General Jorge Ubico, who had granted it total exemption from internal taxes, duty-free import privileges, and a guarantee of low wages. The secretary's brother Allen, head of the Central Intelligence Agency, had been on the company's board. Undersecretary of State W. Bedell Smith, while discussing the company's affairs with Thomas G. Corcoran, its Washington lobbyist, had expressed the hope of becoming its president, and after leaving government he was to be made a member of its board. The family of Henry Cabot Lodge, former senator and now ambassador to the United Nations, owned United Fruit Company stock, while John Moors Cabot, assistant secretary of state for inter-American affairs, was the brother of Thomas Cabot, who served for a time as the company's president.[99] According to Eisenhower's memoirs, it was John Moors Cabot who convinced him that Guatemala was "playing the Communist game."[100]

In the late summer of 1953 Kermit Roosevelt, reporting at the White House on the Central Intelligence Agency operation he had directed in Iran, which had resulted in the overthrow of Prime Minister Muhammad Mussadegh, observed that Secretary Dulles seemed to find special pleasure in what he was hearing. Suspecting that Dulles was contemplating something further along the same lines, Roosevelt saw fit to warn those assembled that such coups would succeed only if they had as their aim something that was wanted also by the army and the people of the country. However, he sensed that Dulles did not want to hear what was being said, for he was still leaning back in his chair with "a catlike grin on his face." Shortly thereafter Kermit Roosevelt was offered command of an undertaking, already under preparation, against the government of Guatemala. However, he decided that the conditions he had suggested did not exist in the case of Guatemala and turned the offer down.[101]

The plan, given final approval late in 1953 or early 1954, was to recruit and support an armed force, to be commanded by a leading Guatemalan, with the expectation that its invasion of Guatemala from a neighboring country would lead to an internal uprising and the overthrow of the Arbenz government.[102] The attackers were to be given air support and receptive officers in the Guatemalan army were to be subverted by means of bribes. Before and during the invasion, the United States would subject Guatemala to harassment, and it would use both overt and covert means to disseminate misinformation designed to put its government in a false light abroad and to create fear and uncertainty within.[103]

The first Guatemalan approached as prospective leader of the invasion force was Miguel Ydígoras Fuentes: as a general under Ubico he had been a zealous enforcer of the compulsory labor laws and in 1950 he had been an unsuccessful candidate against Arbenz.[104] Ydígoras was receptive to the offer but unwilling to accept conditions that accompanied it, and the CIA finally settled on Carlos Castillo Armas, who had led an unsuccessful coup against Arévalo in 1949.[105] The invasion force, consisting of a few hundred Guatemalan exiles and mercenaries, was assembled on a United Fruit Company plantation in Honduras and on one of Somoza's estates in Nicaragua, while a number of transport and combat planes, including three bombers, were flown in under the guise of military assistance to the two countries.[106] The CIA set up a dummy arms company in the United States through which to send infantry weapons to the "Liberation Army" it was assembling. It also gathered together some weapons with Soviet markings to be planted in Guatemala just before the invasion: they were intended later to be "discovered," in substantiation of charges that the Soviet Union had been trying to establish a foothold in the country.[107]

On 13 June Carlos Castillo Armas went to Tegucigalpa to meet for the first time the force of Guatemalan exiles, Central American mercenaries, and American soldiers of fortune that he was to command, and five days later he led them across the frontier and into Guatemala. About the same time men and arms were loaded onto several schooners for an attack on Puerto Barrios. Castillo Armas's first objective was Zacapa, connected by rail with both Puerto Barrios and Guatemala City and situated about twenty miles from the border. However, by the time his force had advanced six miles, he was instructed to stay put, avoid battles, and await further instructions. Within Guatemala there had been no rising of the populace, the army had not mutinied, and campesinos were surrounding and occupying United Fruit Company lands. Local civil guards had captured one of the munitions ships, and though the other vessels unloaded men and arms, the invaders failed to take Puerto Barrios.[108]

The success of the plan to overthrow Arbenz now depended on what could be accomplished through air attacks. Guatemala, with only training planes of pre–World War II vintage, could mount no defense in the air. Nevertheless, almost everything went wrong from the start. Several planes carried out bombing and strafing attacks, but a pilot sent to knock out the government radio station, and given a vivid description of an American missionary building down the street he was to be careful about, got the message turned around and hit the wrong building. Another pilot failed to watch his fuel gauge and had to crash land over the border in Mexico. Worst of all, two of the three bombers were put out of commission by small arms fire.[109]

On 21 June, as Allen Dulles and his staff were debating what to do next, the government of Guatemala appealed to the United Nations. Ambassador Lodge, whose turn it was in June to serve as president of the Security Council, at first resisted the efforts of Secretary General Dag Hammarskjöld to have it called into session, but finally agreed to have a meeting scheduled for 25 June, a full week after the invasion had begun. Lodge also informed the White House that Great Britain and France were preparing to back a proposal for the Security Council to send observers to Central America. It happened that Churchill and Eden were just then beginning a White House visit, where Eisenhower and Dulles lobbied them unmercifully, with the consequence that Great Britain abstained on the motion; France followed suit, and the proposal failed to pass.[110]

In Washington the time gained by these maneuvers was used for the purpose of gaining authorization for sending replacements for the bombers that had been put out of commission. U.S. participation was supposed to be covert and deniable, but with the entire focus on air operations, the appearance of replacement planes would raise the question of where they could come from, if not from the United States. At the White House Eisenhower asked Allen Dulles what the operation's chances would be, with the replacement planes or without them, and Dulles replied that without them the chances would be about zero, and with them about 20 percent. Eisenhower decided to approve sending the planes, and the operation went ahead.[111]

When the new planes became available the CIA pilots went on a bombing and strafing rampage, and with their support Castillo managed to capture the town of Chiquimula, upward of twenty-five miles from the Honduran border. With a few dozen killed or wounded on each side, it was the bloodiest battle of the invasion, and it marked the deepest penetration of Guatemala achieved by rebel forces. But a clandestine CIA radio station, using the same channel as the government station, presented a picture of fearsome battles, Guatemalan defeats, and rebel columns gathering recruits as they advanced. This misinformation was believed, in part, because the international press corps—barred from the "war zone"—accepted what it was being told at the American Embassy and by the press office of the United Fruit Company.[112] Meanwhile, Guatemala City itself was being raided, with the psychological effect of one night raid heightened by the playing of a tape recording of a bombing attack over loudspeakers mounted on the American Embassy roof.[113]

On 27 June residents of Guatemala City, hearing radio reports of the proximity of heavily armed rebel columns and believing that a battle for control of the capital was imminent, began fleeing from the city. That same day a CIA pilot, learning of the presence in the Pacific port of San José of a cargo ship and somehow convinced that it had a cargo of gasoline for Guatemala's army, put a bomb down its smokestack as it stood taking on cargo. As it happened, it had brought no gasoline, and fortunately no lives were lost, but the sinking suggested that the Americans might be intending to deprive Guatemala of its access to foreign markets. On that day, too, the army chief of staff informed Arbenz that a group of leading officers intended to demand his resignation. Convinced that the Americans were intent on his removal from office and that he no longer could count on the army, Arbenz instructed Guillermo Toriello, his foreign minister, to ascertain the U.S. Embassy's surrender terms.

Calling on Ambassador John Peurifloy, Toriello asked whether he would have the fighting stopped if a military junta took control. Would Arbenz have to leave office, Toriello asked, and would his own resignation do any good? Peurifloy, though he had been one of the directors of the unfolding drama, claimed that he had no control over events and no ability to speak for the insurgent forces. He did say, however, that he thought the situation called for a clean sweep.

That evening Arbenz broadcast a farewell speech over the government radio station, saying he was leaving the administration in the care of Colonel Enrique Díaz, the armed forces chief of staff, and shortly before midnight he walked to the Mexican Embassy, across the street from the National Palace, where he was given asylum.[114]

Colonel Díaz, Peurifloy found, was unwilling to have any dealings with Castillo Armas. Díaz also proposed to issue a general amnesty and free all political prisoners, and this would have included leading Communists, who had been taken into custody the day before at Peurifloy's suggestion so that they could not "mobilize forces." Peurifloy was outraged, called in another air raid on the capital, and thus forced Díaz to step down in favor of a Colonel Elfegio Monzon, who was willing to deal with Castillo.[115]

Peurifloy arranged for Monzon to meet in El Salvador with Castillo, and after their negotiations had been completed had Castillo flown to Guatemala City in the embassy plane, which arrived accompanied by an escort that included nine fighter air-craft.[116] He took the position of provisional president on 8 July 1954, and five days later the United States granted official rec-ognition to his government. At about this same time Secretary Dulles instructed Peurifloy to ensure that Castillo made gener-ous arrangements with the United Fruit Company, and it re-ceived the return of all its expropriated lands.[117] In addition, Castillo canceled the land reform law, returned the other ex-propriated holdings, and abolished not only the General Con-federation of Guatemalan Workers, which had communist leadership, but also the non-communist General Confederation of Guatemalan Peasants.[118] With U.S. government help he drew up a new Petroleum Code that removed the prohibition on foreign concessions. Under it, American corporations were granted exploration rights covering over four million hectares. During the first weeks of Castillo Armas's regime, there were many summary executions. He brought back Ubico's secret police chief and restored him to his former post, and the new government instituted many repressive measures.[119]

Colonel Castillo Armas was assassinated, apparently by a member of his own bodyguard and for reasons that remain un-known, three years after he had come to power, and was suc-ceeded by General Ydígoras Fuentes. In 1960 the CIA ap-proached the latter for a place where it could have training bases built and airstrips laid down in preparation for the planned invasion of Castro's Cuba. Ydígoras agreed, and a large planta-tion was made available for American use. The relevant plan-ning was highly classified and the Guatemalan army command was not consulted about the project, but the preparations for the invasion could not be kept secret. With large amounts of cargo coming in through the capital's airport, army officers soon learned that alien forces were being assembled and trained on Guatemalan soil for the purpose of overthrowing Castro.[120]

On 13 November 1960 about 120 officers—their sense of nationalism offended, resentful over not having been consulted, some of them admirers of Castro as a Cuban nationalist—staged an uprising in Guatemala City. Leading about half the army, they were joined by others who seized Puerto Barrios on the coast and the barracks at Zacapa, halfway between there and Guatemala City. At Zacapa, according to one account, hundreds of peasants converged on the barracks asking for arms with which to join the fight against the government, but the rebelling officers could not make up their minds to arm the peasants. Meanwhile, the United States responded to the danger that the Cuban operation would be upset by intervening to help put the rebellion down. A number of CIA bombers, piloted by Cuban exiles, were sent to attack rebel positions, and with their help loyal troops defeated the rebel forces.[121]

The punishment in the countries of Central America for having engaged in an unsuccessful revolt ordinarily was not severe—stiff lectures, demotions, and periods of confinement to barracks—and Guatemala was no exception. Nevertheless, some of the officers, remembering the offers of many peasants to join in their revolt, chose not to take their punishment, but rather to take to the hills and wage a guerrilla struggle against the government. The most important of these groups, led by young officers who had been trained by the United States at Fort Benning and in the Canal Zone, issued a call for a national rebellion against what they termed a regime of "tyranny and humiliation" and for the establishment of a government "which represents human rights, seeks ways . . . to save our country from its hardships, and pursues a self-respecting foreign policy." Shortly afterward another group took to the field under the leadership of the Arbenz administration's defense minister, and it issued a similar call.[122]

During the almost quarter of a century following this beginning of insurgency, Guatemala had as its presidents an army colonel and five generals. The leaders of the first guerrilla bands were killed, their bands were decimated, and it appeared for a time that the government's counterinsurgency operations, conducted with the benefit of U.S. training and material support, had been entirely successful.[123] But it was a government that made enemies of its people. A new guerrilla movement drew in the remnants of previous insurgencies, and soon there were four Marxist-oriented insurgent organizations. One of them was composed largely of Maya Indians—a people who had generally held aloof from politics, but were reacting against seizures of their lands. These bands operated principally in the countryside, but they also from time to time carried out assassinations and kidnappings in urban centers.[124]

In the countryside the renewed counterinsurgency carried on by the government took the lives of many peasants: nobody really knew how many, but a study undertaken by Guatemala's Supreme Court put the number of children who had lost either one parent or both at 110,000. In addition, many peasants became refugees, some 150,000 of them across the border in Mexico.[125] In urban centers, in dealing with actual and suspected sources of opposition, the regime depended on a policy of terrorism. Over a period of twenty years, death squads connected with the army and the police abducted, in some cases tortured, and killed some tens of thousands of people. The first victims, besides Communists, were people who had merely supported Arévalo and Arbenz. The attention of the death squads was then extended to students, trade unionists, and professional people who had organized to protest injustices.[126] In 1979, the United States having urged that political participation not be confined to right-wing parties, the Guatemalan government encouraged the Social Democrats to register their party as one that intended to participate in elections. Thereafter, however, its principal leaders were one after another hunted down and killed.[127]

In many instances people seized by squads of right-wing terrorists vanished without a trace, and a committee made up of relatives of such people composed dossiers on their cases. Formed in 1970, but dissolved after its founder was killed, it succeeded in documenting 15,325 cases during the four years of its existence. Another such organization, which called itself the "Mutual Support Group for the Appearance Alive of Our Children, Spouses, Brothers and Sisters," was formed in 1984.

The following year, President Oscar Humberto Mejía Victores declared: "To take steps toward the reappearance alive of the disappeared is a subversive act, and measures will be adopted to deal with it." A few days later one of the few male leaders of the organization was taken into custody by men in civilian clothes. His mutilated body was later found where it had been dumped beside a road.[128]

By 1985 the leaders of numerous Latin American countries, and the prime minister of Spain as well, had appealed to the military of Guatemala to return the country to civilian rule. The time for these appeals was well chosen. The country was suffering from the worst economic crisis in its history, and despite the repression, there were riots in the capital. These were the circumstances under which the military allowed the election, and the inauguration early in 1986, of President Marco Vinicio Cerezo Arévalo, a leader of the Social Democratic Party who had somehow survived three attempts on his life by rightist death squads.[129]

The United Fruit Company had long since disappeared from the scene, merged with another corporation, which had transferred its operations to Honduras,[130] but vast acreages of hacienda lands still stood idle—and this in a country where 90 percent of the farms were too small to support a family, where three hundred thousand peasants had no land at all, and where people were dying of malnutrition.[131] President Cerezo did not need to be told that taxing idle lands would give the owners incentive to bring them under cultivation, increase opportunities for employment and the availability of foodstuffs, and provide the government with needed revenue. However, in 1986, faced with landowner opposition, he postponed attempts to initiate such taxation. Instead, he promised the peasantry that the government, during the ensuing year, would buy and distribute enough unused lands to support seventy thousand peasants.[132] Subsequently, evidently encouraged by Cerezo's intention to address the fundamental problem of landlessness and hunger, the guerrilla organizations expressed a readiness for negotiations to end the insurgency.[133] There remained a wide gulf between the insurgents and the military, however, and Vinicio Cerezo's rule depended on the sufferance of the armed forces: as one leader of the army declared, "Vinicio is a project of ours—not Vinicio himself, but the return to civilian institutions." [134]

We have now considered the case of Cuba, in the context of its demands upon Spain, first for reforms, and, after promise of reforms had been only partially kept, for independence. I have also recounted the experiences of Cuba, of Nicaragua, and of Guatemala in their relations with the United States, experiences that offended their sense of national self-respect or resulted in the setting aside of needed reforms, if not both. Considered together, they illustrate the workings in practice of the generalizations set forth at the beginning of this chapter: if the problems that gave rise to them are fundamental, causes that have been defeated or suppressed are likely to reemerge; and by passing through a cycle of suppression and reemergence, such causes are likely to become radicalized.

2 The Rural and Popular Nature of Wars of the Third Kind

It is in the rural areas of the underdeveloped lands of the so-called Third World, and only in such lands, that wars of the third kind take place. This is supported, first of all, by the historic record. Napoleon won victory after victory in countries to the north and east of France, and by 1808 he was apparent master of Europe. That year he invaded economically backward Spain in what he intended to be a campaign of quick decision. It lasted seven years and tied down a French army that came to number 320,000. Napoleon's forces easily shattered the Spanish armies; it was the numerous guerrilla bands, made up largely of peasants, that made the occupation of Spain a disaster.[1]

Our own times have provided no record of guerrilla wars, as distinguished from campaigns of terrorism, in the developed countries of Western Europe and North America. In the period of the Korean War, during which the United States used Japan as a logistic base, the Japanese Communist Party—acting in response to Chinese communist instigation—set up what were intended to be guerrilla bases in the Japanese countryside, but none of them lasted more than the briefest time.[2] However, since the end of World War II, wars of the third kind have broken out in such countries as Afghanistan, Algeria, Angola, Burma, Cambodia, China, Cuba, El Salvador, Ethiopia, Guatemala, Malaya, Nicaragua, the Philippines, and Vietnam.

As demonstrated by this list, a country suited to the conduct of a war of the third kind may constitute a continuous area of almost any size and shape, or an archipelago. It may be in the temperate zone or in the tropics, mountainous or flat, forested or open, uniform in its features or of varied terrain. The populace may be homogeneous or diverse, and the people of the countryside may live either in scattered dwellings or in villages. Such particulars, as we shall see, may be expected to have a bearing on the course, duration, and outcome of such wars, but none represents a precondition to their occurrence. What each country had was an underdeveloped and predominantly rural economy, the kind of economy in which agriculture, animal husbandry, and handicraft production are for home consumption and sale on local markets, and in which the people of the countryside lead largely self-sufficient lives.

The reason wars of the third kind require such an environment arises from the way a guerrilla force must be supported. A regular army in the field must receive from its home base and over its line of communications the personnel replacements it needs and the quantities of matériel such a force consumes. A force engaged in guerrilla warfare, the refuge of the militarily weak, may be composed of the remnants of an army that has had such logistic support but lost it consequent to inability to defend its territorial base and line of communications; or, made up of rebels, it may never have had such advantages to lose. Because the hit-and-run operations of a guerrilla force are suited only to light weapons, and because they usually involve brief periods of combat, guerrillas may be able to get along largely with the arms and ammunition they are able to capture. But the inability of a guerrilla force to defend a base area and line of communications in positional warfare means that it must depend for food, recruits, intelligence, and hiding places directly upon the people of the region in which it operates. This direct and immediate dependence on the populace is what makes guerrilla forces different from regular armies, whose support by the people is at a remove and has their government as intermediary. It also serves to differentiate guerrillas from raiding commandos and from partisans operating in conjunction with regular armies and dependent upon such armies for logistic support.

A guerrilla force must find safety from its more powerful

opponent through dispersal that prevents the enemy from finding, fixing, and fighting it on its own terms. It is a principle
that should be obvious, even had it not been emphasized by
Clausewitz, that victory is most likely to be won if one's own
forces can be concentrated against inferior parts of the enemy
or other decisive objectives in the theater of war. It might be
added that concentration comes naturally to regular armies because they are most readily quartered, fed, supplied, transported, and maneuvered in units of substantial size. In a developed country the loss of the capital and other principal cities,
paralyzing government and disrupting the economy, must necessarily be followed by the surrender or destruction of its
armed forces. Accordingly, those forces have no choice but to
stand and defend their country's strategic centers, and they
must also protect the umbilical cord represented by their line of
communications.

The irregular forces of an underdeveloped land are under no
comparable compulsion. In nineteenth-century Russia, Field
Marshal Ivan Paskevich, considered a military genius, proposed to Nicholas I a plan for the conquest of the Caucasus that
envisioned the seizure of strategic points. His proposal, however, was demolished by General Aleksei Veliaminov, who
demonstrated that for the tribespeople of the Caucasus there
were no such points. In addition, because each horseman could
meet his immediate needs from what he carried, the forces that
opposed the Russians had no need to defend a line of communications or protect a baggage train, either of which would
have been vulnerable to Russian attack. In this situation the
Russians, superior in numbers and armament, long found themselves unable to compel the resistance forces of the Caucasus to
risk destruction in battles of position. Indeed, the conflict against
the particularly stubborn tribesmen of Dagestan and Tchetchnia, led by Imam Shamil, dragged on for over twenty years.[3]
Their case simply demonstrates the rule, which might be illustrated by no end of other conflicts of the same kind, that a successful guerrilla resistance implies the absence of the need to defend strategic centers or vital lines of communication.

The rule that calls for concentrating superior forces of one's
own against inferior units of the enemy is nevertheless appli-

cable to guerrillas, as it is to their opponents, but within a context of much more limited scale and duration. Mao Zedong unquestionably had this in mind when he wrote to his party's headquarters in Shanghai that he and Zhu De were using guerrilla tactics, dividing their forces to work among the people but concentrating them to deal with the enemy. The concentration of the communist forces, he implied, was on a limited scale and within an overall context of dispersion: in likening dispersal and concentration to spreading a net wide and drawing it in again, Mao observed that the radius involved was relatively short.[4] Observing the principle of concentrating superior forces of one's own against inferior forces of the enemy obviously implies that one should avoid engagements with superior forces of the enemy. In later years, talking of how he and his comrades had conducted guerrilla warfare, Mao Zedong bluntly declared: "We ran away." Nathanael Greene said much the same thing about the conduct of the war in the South during the American Revolution. However, perhaps remembering the sixty-mile flight from the scene of the battle of Camden by his predecessor Horatio Gates, Greene added: "But I have taken care not to run too far."

It follows in logic from the inability of guerrillas to defend important centers and lines of communication, and from their own need to find safety through dispersal, that the sources of support on which they depend must be widely available rather than concentrated. In underdeveloped agrarian lands, the bulk of the population will be found in the countryside, and the nature of their agricultural and pastoral pursuits ensures that they will live dispersed in individual homesteads or small villages. Because production in such countries is mostly for home use and for sale in nearby markets, foodstuffs and other basic necessities will be locally available in much of the countryside. Thus the rural areas of such lands contain the sources of recruits, food, and other necessities, all widely dispersed, that a guerrilla force must have. Usually drawn at least in part from the rural populace, a guerrilla force also should be able to look to it for intelligence concerning opposing forces and for the means of concealment and evasion it needs if it is to survive and prosper. It was the widespread availability of such forms of support in the Caucasus prior to its incorporation in the Russian empire, to cite but one relevant example, that enabled horsemen from the Caucasus to raid across the Russian border with near impunity. As one of his generals explained to Nicholas I, the tribesmen in returning from a raid had no need to keep to any given direction and, once across the frontier, could find food and shelter anywhere they might go.[5]

The developed countries are unsuited to the support of guerrillas for reasons that include the fact that the proportion of the population living in the countryside is generally small. In addition, agricultural production in such lands is primarily specialized and destined for distant markets, rather than diversified and suitable for direct consumption, and home industries and their products are generally lacking. As Mao Zedong observed, it would have been impossible for the Chinese Communists to have built and maintained their guerrilla armies in rural China if that country had had a unified capitalist economy rather than a localized agricultural one.[6]

In appreciating why the developed countries are not suited to be theaters for wars of the third kind, it may also be useful to recall a fact so fundamental that it is likely to remain below the level of consideration by public officials and private citizens of highly structured societies: those who govern cannot deal with those they govern on a purely one-to-one basis; a people must be aggregated if they are to be governed. Sun Yat-sen had this in mind when he likened the people of prerevolutionary China to a sheet of sand and advanced his Three People's Principles in the hope that they would serve to bind the Chinese people together in the republican cause.

In highly developed countries the aggregating factors include the circumstances under which people work and live. It is not only a matter of the physical concentration of a high proportion of the inhabitants in cities, facilitating the exercise over them of police power and other means of direct control. In addition, there is the fact that a city's residents are crucially dependent for their day-to-day living on the power plants, waterworks, food stores, banks, and other sources of goods and services the city contains. These serve to aggregate a city's residents, and hence to provide means whereby they can be controlled indirectly and en masse. And because agriculture in developed countries is generally specialized production for the market, typically devoted in any particular region to only one or a few crops, and because the range of needs of those engaged in specialized agriculture will be much the same as that of city dwellers, the dependence of the rural populace on the facilities of urban centers—if perhaps less immediate than is the case with city dwellers—will be similar. Accordingly, those who hold the cities of a developed country hold the keys to the control of its people.

Where, then, are the keys to control of countries in which the facilities and services we associate with urban centers are largely lacking, and in which most of the people depend on subsistence agriculture and animal husbandry, handicraft production, home industries, and the sale of surpluses in nearby markets? In such countries the people of rural areas can, if necessary, get along indefinitely without access to urban centers, but the inhabitants of the towns and cities depend on the surrounding countryside for the foodstuffs essential to day-to-day living. The keys to the control of these economically unadvanced countries, which usually are underdeveloped administratively as well, remain in urban centers only so long as the countryside does not fall under hostile control. This vulnerability was demonstrated in the early months of 1915 when, by shutting off the capital's food supplies, rebel Zapatistas in control of Mexico City's countryside forced the occupying army of Álvaro Obregón to abandon the city to them.[7] The control of rural areas is thus crucial to the governments of underdeveloped countries. It was Mao Zedong's early recognition of that fact, when others were blind to it, and the strategic concepts he derived from the insight that constituted his crucial contribution to the success of the Chinese Communists' long struggle to gain power and that entitle him to a place in the first rank among modern revolutionary thinkers.

However, even in underdeveloped countries, the cities represent an environment inhospitable to guerrillas. Discussing the Philippines' post–World War II Hukbalahap rebellion, its leader Luis Taruc observed that in a rural barrio everyone knew everybody else, but that in Manila one's house might be passed all day long by strangers, any one of whom might be a spy. The city, he said, was too confined a space for guerrillas, and block raids were too hard to dodge.[8] The Chinese Communists, particularly during the early years of their long struggle for power, tried to take major cities by uprisings from within synchronized with attacks from without; at Canton the attempt ended in a disastrous defeat and a bloody purge, but in most cases there were no uprisings at all. Indeed, it was not until the last year of the civil war, conducted intermittently for twenty-one years, that the Chinese Communists were able to take and hold major cities in intramural China.[9]

Among rebellions that were largely urban-based, one of the more instructive was that waged by Uruguay's Tupamaro National Liberation Front, whose heyday was the late 1960s and the early 1970s. Upward of half the people of Uruguay live in Montevideo; in much of the country there are many cattle and sheep, but few people; and a popular rebellion must be waged where the people are. The Tupamaros found that maintaining the necessary secrecy in an urban environment made it difficult to gain recruits and other forms of support on the scale required for a broadly based resistance movement. Unable to solve the contradiction between the requirements of a clandestine existence and the need for mass support, the Tupamaros fell back on acts of terrorism—kidnappings for ransom, bank robberies, bombings, and assassination—and once a decisive campaign to eradicate them was undertaken, they were quickly suppressed.[10]

When China's Cultural Revolution spilled over into Hong Kong during the 1960s and Chinese radicals tried to take the colony over from within, the often indiscriminate acts of violence perpetrated by terrorists in crowded streets and other public places, besides claiming bystanders as well as intended victims, created an atmosphere of fear and feelings of revulsion among the people at large. In addition, acts of sabotage against public utilities and other enterprises deprive the populace of essential services and of necessary employment. In the case of Hong Kong, the acts of the terrorists alienated the inhabitants—although 98 percent of them, like the terrorists, were

Chinese—and helped make it possible for the British-led police to root out the terrorists from their various strongholds.

Similarly, during the post–World War II insurgency in Malaya—referred to by the British as the Emergency—Chinese terrorists alienated the predominantly Chinese populace of Singapore by such indiscriminate acts of violence as the dynamiting of randomly chosen street cars, in which numerous people were killed and injured.[11] This case, like those of Montevideo and Hong Kong, provides support by negative example for the propositions that guerrillas cannot be city-based and that the designation "urban guerrilla" is a contradiction in terms.

In sum, wars of the third kind are wars in which the support of one side is drawn not from a government and along a line of communications, but directly from the people of the country in which the two sides fight. It is only the rural areas of underdeveloped countries that provide environments suitable for the conduct of such wars. Attempts to conduct them in developed countries have been unsuccessful, and efforts to extend them to urban centers have degenerated into self-defeating campaigns of terror.

3 *Organization and Motivation*

It would seem self-evident that unified direction of insurgencies and effective mobilization of their support require that there be organizations devoted to those purposes. In actual practice, some insurgencies, particularly, wars of resistance, have been fought with a paucity of organization matching their poverty of material means, which leaders accustomed to the requirements of conventional armies might find incomprehensible. Others, notably ones led by Marxist-Leninists, have been characterized by organizational effort that can only be called prodigious.

That there can be such a range of possibilities between the little and the highly organized is owing to the circumstance that the factors of organization and cause, in substantial measure though never completely, are interchangeable variables. Less organizational effort is needed on behalf of causes many people share in common, to which they readily react, and about which they feel deeply; more effort, perhaps involving a substantial measure of compulsion, may be required to produce the desired response if the cause is divisive or arouses limited spontaneous enthusiasm. The cause that may be expected to evoke the strongest and most uniform response, especially in the present age of nationalisms, is that of independence from external domination. The response of a populace to those engaged in armed uprisings against their own government is likely to be ambivalent, especially to the extent that their evident aims are revolutionary rather than merely reformist.

The organizational means whereby rebellions and wars of resistance are directed and supported are commonly called their infrastructures, though the term may be deceptive, suggesting an articulation that is likely to be lacking. The concentration usual in conventional armies facilitates the exercise over them of centralized command and their support over well-defined lines of communication; the dispersion characterizing guerrillas and the populace upon which they depend requires decentralization of command over forces and of control over their sources of support. This decentralization is feasible only within the context of a considerable measure of self-discipline on the part of guerrillas, and voluntarism in the case of their supporters. The essential element to the unified direction of decentralized operations is commitment to a common cause on the part of both leadership and followers. More often than not the cause has a component of nationalism, which tends to ensure that these movements will be unresponsive to efforts to bring them under foreign control.

Guerrilla bases, which may be defined as areas from which guerrillas draw their support, are generally not defensible against determined attack. Access to foreign territory as sanctuary and as source of support, however useful, cannot serve as a complete substitute for internal support. Indeed, forces that depend entirely on foreign support should be classified as raiders rather than guerrillas and, depending on the degree of complicity on the part of countries that give them sanctuary and support, as agents of external aggression. Although a third party may gain political capital by assisting one of two sides, such capital is likely to prove highly perishable. Finally, the organizational aspects of wars of the third kind may have an importance transcending that of the wars themselves, for structures created to lead and support them may be the subsequent peacetime governments in embryo.

Decentralization

The general headquarters or other authority to which guerrilla or other irregular forces may be subordinate can set forth the objectives it wants them to attain and lay down the operational and other policies it wants them to follow. But commanders in the field are necessarily allowed a substantial degree of operational autonomy: no general headquarters could make detailed decisions for numerous small units scattered about it knows not where, in circumstances of which it may be unaware, on behalf of commanders who may have to act as fast as they can think. That being so, one can understand why American visitors to Yenan during World War II found that Zhu De, the communist commander in chief, had no map room, possessed only a general idea as to the disposition of his forces, and—like other top leaders in Yenan—seemed to have plenty to time to talk with foreign visitors. One can also believe the truth of the assertion of one of his commanders in the field that he did not send telegraphic requests to Yenan because they were never answered.[1] The decentralization of command over communist forces implied a similar decentralization of control over their support organization, and the field commanders had to look to it for support rather than to headquarters at Yenan.

The hit-and-run war of the guerrilla cannot be conducted by men who are serving unwillingly and whose discipline depends predominantly on fear of their commanding officers, for such men cannot be depended on to regroup after flight in order to fight another day. The fact that irregular forces must be able to melt away and subsequently to regroup implies a measure of voluntarism arising from commitment to their cause. Seth Warner depended on the self-imposed discipline of his New England militiamen, surrounded by British troops during Burgoyne's invasion from Canada, when he issued the order: "Scatter and meet me in Manchester." They did, and subsequently were on hand to help defeat Burgoyne's Hessians at the Battle of Bennington.[2] And what is true of guerrillas' commitment to a cause must also be true of those who give them support, for guerrillas, when in a tight spot, can seek safety in flight, whereas their supporters, tied to their homes and herds, cannot follow suit.

Wars of Resistance

Guerrilla resistance to the armed forces of a foreign country is likely to begin in a context of political and military disorganization arising in the wake of the destruction of the regular army of the invaded country, and perhaps of its government as well. In such circumstances the means of providing well-organized direction and support to the resistance will at least temporarily be lacking. However, as should be readily appreciated by all, but is not, few causes can evoke more widespread and deeply felt response than resistance to a foreign invader or alien oppressor. Accordingly, spontaneity of response by the populace, with many people taking up arms and others readily giving them support, can largely make up for deficient organization and make a stubborn resistance possible. Insofar as the need for organization is concerned, wars of resistance thus stand at the lower end of the scale.

That was true, for example, of the Spanish resistance to Napoleon during the 1807–14 Peninsular War. Charles IV and his son Ferdinand became captives of Napoleon and were forced to leave Spain in 1808. By the end of that year the regular armies of Spain had virtually ceased to exist. The following year the first guerrilla bands appeared. They were nominally under the supervision of a central revolutionary junta and of juntas formed for the various provinces, which did help the guerrillas in small ways, monetary for the most part, and called on the people to give the guerrillas food, other supplies, and information. However, the juntas were chased from town to town by the French, squabbled among themselves, and were too disorganized to act as an alternative government.[3]

Indeed, the guerrillas were a law unto themselves, and the people did not wait to be told to support them. Guerrilla warfare, in which every man might feel he was his own commander, suited the individualism of the Spanish temperament, and though there necessarily were leaders, they were not a caste apart. Indeed, according to J. F. A. Lemière de Corvey, one of the principal officers of Napoleon's army, the outstanding leaders were "a miller, doctor, shepherd, curate, some monks, a few deserters, but not a single man of mark before that time."[4] All the inhabitants served as spies to their fellow citizens, he declared, and thus the guerrillas could join together to be at least twice the enemy's number. Thus, in the course of the Peninsular War, between one hundred fifty and two hundred guerrilla bands, without fighting a single pitched battle, took the lives of half a million French soldiers.[5] "These guerrillas," a military commentator of that period wrote, "carried their basis in themselves, as it were, and every operation against them terminated in the disappearance of its object."[6]

The final liberation of Spain from the French armies owed something also to regular forces operating in the Iberian Peninsula under the Duke of Wellington, and it came only after defeats that Napoleon suffered elsewhere, notably at the hands of Russian irregulars and Russian winter. But Spain had been a bleeding ulcer, and Napoleon evidently traced to it the defeats he suffered elsewhere. At any rate, after Waterloo, in exile on St. Helena, he declared: "It was that miserable Spanish affair that killed me."[7]

In more recent times, the guerrilla phase of the so-called Philippine Insurrection similarly began in a context of great disorganization, for the 50,000-man Filipino army had been defeated and disbanded and the officials of the Malolos government were isolated in the mountains of northern Luzon, where they had taken refuge. In such circumstances, support for continued resistance to U.S. forces depended on local Filipino leaders and the populace at large. The pervasiveness of that support surprised American leaders, who perhaps had not paid attention to cables sent to the State Department by the American consul at Manila shortly before the outbreak of the Spanish-American War. The Spanish authorities in the Philippines had been trying in vain, he reported, to suppress an independence movement like the one in Cuba.[8]

The Filipinos themselves were in hardly a good position to create an organized basis for the support of a guerrilla resistance, but the invading Americans, in appointing local officials, inadvertently did it for them. Describing Filipino support for that resistance some months after it had begun, General Adna Romanza Chafee reported: "Throughout these islands, wherever a *presidente* of a *pueblo* or *cabeza* of a *barrio* was appointed or elected under American authority, he, with few exceptions, either acted in the same capacity for the insurgents or maintained silence with respect to his neighbor who served in like

capacity in the same jurisdiction." Discussing the behavior of
such officials, General Arthur MacArthur wrote:

> In all matters touching the peace of the town, the regulation of mar-
> kets, the primitive work possible on roads, streets and bridges, and the
> institution of schools, their open activity was commendable; at the
> same time they were exacting and collecting contributions and sup-
> plies and recruiting men for the Filipino forces, and sending all avail-
> able military information to the Filipino leaders. Wherever through-
> out the archipelago there is a group of the insurgent army, it is a fact
> beyond dispute, that all contiguous towns contribute to the mainte-
> nance thereof . . . not only so in the sense of furnishing supplies for
> the so-called flying columns of the guerrillas, but as affording secure
> places of refuge. Indeed, it is now the most important maxim of Fili-
> pino tactics to disband when closely pressed and seek safety in the near-
> est barrio; a maneuver quickly accomplished by reason of the assistance
> of the people and the ease with which the Filipino soldier is trans-
> formed into the appearance of a peaceful native.[9]

The conclusions concerning popular support for wars of
resistance that may be drawn from conflicts such as the Peninsular War and the Philippine Insurrection have a relevance extending beyond outright wars of conquest. Foreign intervention in such conflicts as that under way in Vietnam in the early
1960s and in Afghanistan beginning in 1979 can give to rebellions and civil wars the additional aspect of wars of resistance
against alien invaders—as the respective difficulties encountered by the United States and the Soviet Union have so amply
shown.

Insurgency: Rebellions and Revolutions

The body politic, which ever tends to reject the implant of a
foreign authority, whatever its pretensions, is relatively tolerant
of domestic misrule. A chief of state is seen first of all in his
representational capacity, which means that his people tend to
identify with him and to overlook his shortcomings. If these
are gross, they nevertheless will say that he is good, but has bad

officials. Accordingly, rebels and revolutionaries, who must draw their support from the same populace as the government, must contend with the ambivalence of popular feeling about opposing a regime that may be bad but is nonetheless their own.

In consequence, an insurgency may be expected to require more effort in the organizational fields of propaganda, recruitment, and material support than a war of resistance. In general, the organizational requirements of a rebellion aimed at gaining a redress of grievances may be expected to be less than those of a revolution directed at achieving a change of government. Most demanding of all—as is reflected in the stress on organization by Marxist-Leninist parties—are revolutions aimed at not only overthrowing a government but at overturning a social order as well. In wars of the third kind, such revolutions may be expected to possess not only military command arrangements and provision of popular support for the revolutionary forces, but also an additional element composed of political and administrative workers, led by party cadres, engaged not only in activities aimed at extending and supporting the revolution but also at providing the basis for the new government to follow.

As already indicated in the context of wars of resistance, organizational arrangements for the support of forces engaged on behalf of a cause that enjoys great popular support may be simple and informal, but yet effective. That may also be true of support arrangements for rebellions aimed at achieving reforms, such as those sought during the 1910–20 Mexican Revolution by the peasants of Morelos and adjoining states. Their cause was that of protecting the communal lands of the villages against continuing encroachment by the haciendas and of recovering lands already taken from them through force and fraud, and their rebellion was conducted against those who were, at any particular time, in charge of the government in Mexico City.[10] The villages, under elected councils of elders, produced bands of armed men, which coalesced under local or regional leaders, with Emiliano Zapata emerging by common consent as their commander in chief.[11] Even after his forces had grown into an army, the villages owed it only the duties of providing its garrisons with farm plots to cultivate, serving as guides and messengers when needed, bringing the troops food and supplies when they were engaged in combat, helping the wounded, and burying the dead.[12]

The Hukbalahap uprising in the Philippines was a case in which an organization adequate for the purpose of conducting a rebellion directed at achieving reforms proved inadequate for carrying the uprising onward toward the goal of revolution. The Hukbalahap was a World War II anti-Japanese guerrilla force with organizational roots in peasant unions that had been built up a few years earlier for the purpose of supporting the rights of tenant farmers. The peasantry, particularly in central Luzon, had been suffering from the ravages of progress, as represented by a shift from diversified agriculture to a cash crop economy. In the process, what had been a cooperative undertaking with shared costs, in which there had been a patriarchal relationship between landlords and tenants, was becoming a more impersonal affair in which the sharecropper lost both the dietary advantages of diversified agriculture and some of his former rights, but none of his former obligations.[13]

After the interregnum of the Japanese occupation, the peasant unions were reestablished and renewed their activities on behalf of the peasantry. The postwar Philippine government, however, responded to their efforts with repression: seven congressmen who were favorable to their cause, elected in the spring of 1946, were denied their seats, and that summer, in an atmosphere of rising tension, a leader of the largest peasant union was abducted by men in military police uniform and killed. The Hukbalahap had been disbanded after liberation, but a number of the leaders of the peasant unions had been Huks, and they responded to armed repression by again taking up arms themselves and reconstituting their wartime organization. In trying to suppress them, the government's forces were guilty of excessive and indiscriminate use of force against the residents of rural barrios, and in consequence the Hukbalahap gained additional recruits.[14]

Luis Taruc, vice president of the largest peasant union and the Hukbalahap supreme commander, was a member of the

Philippine Communist Party (PKP), as were a number of other Huk leaders, but they were men of a certain independence, who were not particularly amenable to Party control.[15] Indeed, in 1946 and 1947 the PKP was engaged in united front politics and opposed to the Huk rebellion. However, in 1948 and 1949, influenced by the fact that the insurgency was gaining force and by the victories of the Chinese Communists on the adjacent Asian mainland, the leadership of the PKP reassessed its position and decided to take command of the rebellion.[16] The name Hukbalahap, an acronym derived from a Tagalog term meaning People's Anti-Japanese Army, was changed to Hukbong Mapagpalaya ng Bayan (HMB), for People's Liberation Army, and José Lava, general secretary of the PKP, became its supreme commander. Taruc was demoted to the chairmanship of one of nine regional committees established in various parts of the country to coordinate the military and support aspects of the rebellion.[17] Subordinate to these were field commands of from one to seven hundred men, ranging in number from seven field commands under Taruc's regional committee for central Luzon to as few as one in distant parts of the archipelago to which PKP leaders had gone on expansion missions. On the support side, the PKP created a pyramidal structure of barrio, section, and district committees, the cadres of which took responsibility for collecting supplies for Huks in the field and for carrying on political work.

On the 29 March 1950 anniversary of the founding of the wartime Hukbalahap, the HMB conducted the raids referred to in the Introduction—simultaneous attacks in all four provinces of central Luzon—and on the 29 August anniversary of the outbreak of the 1896 revolution against Spain, it again raided a number of urban centers, among them a provincial capital not far from Manila, where the Huks looted the municipal treasury.[18]

Up to this point it was the Philippine Constabulary, an arm of the Interior Ministry, that had the responsibility for suppressing the rebellion. Its relations with the people were not helped by the fact that many of the constabulary's men had been in it during World War II, when it had served the occupying Japanese army. And since its reestablishment in the immediate postwar period, as already noted, it had become widely hated in the countryside for its abuse of the rural populace.[19]

It was in the immediate wake of the 29 August 1950 raids that President Elpidio Quirino appointed Ramon Magsaysay to the post of secretary of national defense. General Mariano Castañeda was superseded as commander of the constabulary, which was placed under the Department of National Defense, and the main responsibility for counterinsurgency operations was assumed by the army.

Magsaysay offered the Huks the choice between all-out force, which soon was being applied with more effectiveness and greater discrimination, or all-out friendship, which meant that those willing to come in from the field were given amnesty and could return to civilian life, in some cases with government resettlement assistance.[20] He got the army deeply involved in civil affairs, and he reached into other parts of the government and out to community organizations for help. Recognizing that the Huk rebellion had roots in the plight of tenant farmers of central Luzon, Magsaysay had young lawyers in the army's Judge Advocate General's Corps represent peasants with grievances in suits against their landlords.[21] Aware of the government's reputation for being responsive only to the well-to-do, he announced that anyone with a grievance against an official, military or civilian, could send him a telegram, for which the equivalent of five cents would be charged, and that an investigation of the grievance would be initiated within twenty-four hours.[22]

The 1949 Philippine elections had been accompanied by much force and fraud, a circumstance that had added fuel to the rebellion. As the 1951 elections approached, the Philippine Veterans Legion and a variety of other civic organizations launched a National Movement for Free Elections. On behalf of the government, Magsaysay announced that the army would guard the polls in order to ensure the freedom of the elections and the safety of civilian election watchers. In fulfillment of this pledge, high school and college ROTC members throughout the archipelago were temporarily blanketed into the army and assigned to duty at the polls. In consequence, the 1951 elections were relatively honest and peaceful, and when the votes were counted, the opposition Nacionalista Party was found to have won the mayoral election in Manila and control of the Senate.[23] As Taruc later said, the effect on the peasants was to "open again elections as alternative to rebellion."[24]

It was in 1951 that the rebellion reached its apogee and began to decline, and for this decline the difference between the respective aims of the Philippine Communist Party and of the peasantry was in no small part responsible. The Party wanted to overthrow the government; the peasants wanted the government to stop its repression. The Party set forth a program calling for far-reaching economic change, whereas the peasant rebels wanted reform of the tenancy system rather than its abolition. The Party proposed to carry the revolution through to the end, but among the peasantry there was widespread weariness of strife. In 1952 the divergence between these two sets of aims and attitudes led to a split in the Party that reached as high as its Political Bureau. That year Taruc and other leaders close to the peasants argued for stopping the fighting and entering into negotiations with the government, and the leaders of some Huk squadrons did so. Some years earlier Taruc had declared: "The Hukbalahap can only hold out as long as it is supported by the masses. No more, no less." In 1953 he said that it no longer had their support, and in 1954 he did what many other Huks had been doing—quit. Thereafter the Huks were reduced to a dwindling number of small bands that no longer posed a peace-and-order problem.[25]

In a base in China's south-central Jiangxi province, built beginning in 1927 under the leadership of Mao Zedong, the Chinese Communists set up a pervasive array of mass organizations, based upon occupation, age, and sex, intended to make possible a complete mobilization of the populace. They began with only a few thousand troops, who happened to have communist commanders, salvaged from the breakup of the Kuomintang-communist alliance against that period's Chinese warlords, and gave them the tasks, besides fighting, of doing propaganda and organizational work among the people. By creating local village guard units and, at the next higher level, guerrilla bands, they established a three-tier military system in which the main forces could call on the part-time fighters in time of need and could draw on them for recruits. As the communist army grew, the Communist Party apparatus within it was expanded and elaborated. In addition, a governmental structure was set up, first at the local and county levels, then culminating in a purported Provisional Central Government.[26] It was intended that the Party should govern through that structure; however, as Mao Zedong admitted, "for the sake of convenience the Party handles many things directly and brushes aside the governmental bodies."[27]

The region in which the Chinese Communists had established their base was a rural one, and there they adopted a policy of land confiscation and redistribution. The implementation of this was accomplished not through bureaucratic means, but by the peasants themselves and to the accompaniment of class struggle, whereby the participants were intended to become irrevocably committed to the communist cause. This involved the holding of "trials" at which landlords were the accused, their tenants and hired laborers the accusers, and the rest of the local people the jury—trials that resulted in the liquidating of the landlords and in making their lands, houses, agricultural implements, and other property available for redistribution. These trials were conducted in an atmosphere of deliberately whipped-up emotion and—because people must hate those whom they wrong—atrocities were sometimes committed not only against landlords but against their families. During the initial years the lands of rich peasants also were confiscated, with compensation taking the form of redistributed land of inferior quality, and this created worry among middle peasants lest they be placed in the rich peasant category. Even those who held only a little land, because they had cared for it and become attached to it, would not be consoled for its loss into the common pool by the hope of a larger and more fertile plot, and all who benefited faced the uncertain prospect of what might happen to them should the area be reconquered by the Kuomintang.[28]

In reporting to the Party Center in Shanghai late in 1928, Mao Zedong had written: "Wherever the Red Army goes, the masses are cold and aloof, and only after our propaganda do they slowly move into action."[29] The Communists' expansion into adjacent areas, though it undoubtedly benefited from enormous efforts in the fields of organization and propaganda, took place under the chilling shadow cast by their socially divisive practices of class struggle. In any case, unable to defend their base against superior Kuomintang armies, the Communists were in 1934 forced to undertake the terrible retreat known as the Long March. In northwestern China, reduced to a tenth of those who had set out, the remnants found refuge in a small guerrilla base that other Communists had created. After taking it over, they established their headquarters in the small town of Yenan and, thanks to the outbreak of the Sino-Japanese War, were able to exchange the divisive policies of their period in Jiangxi for the unifying cause of national resistance.

Subsequent to the founding in 1949 of the People's Republic of China, Mao Zedong in effect admitted that the Chinese Communists might not have been able to win the civil war had they not postponed their land revolution in favor of the anti-Japanese united front. To a Japanese visitor who expressed regret over Japan's past aggression against China, Mao declared that there was no need for apologies. Rather, Mao said, the Chinese Communists should thank the Japanese, for it was their invasion that had enabled the Chinese Communists to lay the basis for their postwar rise to power.[30]

The anti-Japanese united front represented a truce of sorts between the two Chinese sides, and with the outbreak of the Sino-Japanese War on 7 July 1937 the government designated the communist forces the Eighth Route Army. Thereafter each fought the Japanese in its own way: the government forces attempted to maintain a conventional defense, the Communists a fluid "war of millet and rifles." Elements of the Eighth Route Army, together with their political workers, moved eastward from the Yenan area and began establishing base areas between and around the transport lines and urban centers of North China on which Japanese logistics depended. In their efforts to mobilize the largely apolitical peasantry, the political cadres of the Eighth Route Army were enormously assisted by the people's experience of mopping-up operations by the Japanese army. (Indeed, in his classic *Peasant Nationalism and Communist Power,* Chalmers Johnson declares that as a general rule the

Communists were able to establish guerrilla bases only in areas that had had direct experience with the Japanese army.)[31]

Because it was economically backward and impoverished, and because the government maintained a blockade against it, the communist territory centered at Yenan could hardly serve as a logistic base for the Eighth Route Army's struggle against the Japanese. Indeed, all that it sent eastward were cadres, recruited from among Chinese who had been attracted to Yenan by the opportunities it afforded for service against the Japanese and who had undergone brief periods of training at Yenan's Resistance University. These cadres joined the political workers of the Eighth Route Army in setting up an array of mass associations based upon occupation, sex, and age—the most numerous being those of peasants, women, and youths, but also including associations of businessmen, teachers, and other middle-class elements. This was much like the activities of the Communists in Jiangxi, but carried on in the far different context of unifying all patriotic elements against the invading Japanese. These mass organizations provided the Communists with a means of aggregating the populace and involving the people in support of the Eighth Route Army: from the membership of the mass associations, they formed supplemental units composed of people who turned from their regular occupations when the need arose to serve as guides, transport workers, stretcher bearers, and nurses. They also drew from these mass associations the recruits for the two lower levels of the three-part military structure—the village militia and the regional guerrillas—on which the main forces could draw for replacements and for expansion. Indeed, by the end of World War II, the Communists' various base areas were supporting main force units totaling between 500,000 and 900,000 men—depending upon whose estimates are accepted—and a far larger number of part-time fighters.[32]

In nineteen base areas, most of them in North China, the Communists set up village and county governments, and in several of them they established regional administrations resembling the provincial governments functioning elsewhere in China. They collected taxes, ran postal systems, controlled a variety of productive enterprises, operated banks and trading

companies, published newspapers, and ran hospitals. Some of
the base areas, no longer dependent on Yenan for a flow of
trained political workers, contained their own cadre schools.
The representatives sent to regional assemblies were chosen
through elections held at local levels, giving the people a sense
of participation, and the services of cooperative officials of the
Kuomintang regime were welcomed.[33] But the mass organizations and government were kept under the control of the Party,
which had grown as the war progressed.[34] By its end the Communists had created what Edgar Snow called "the largest guerrilla organization in the world."[35] In addition, they were leading governments ruling approximately 100,000,000 people and
that anticipated the establishment in 1949 of the People's Republic of China.[36]

Political Control of Revolutionary Forces

Revolutions have their own dynamics, making it peculiarly
difficult to conduct them under the control of a unified leadership. The most readily fractured is the relationship between the
political heads of a revolutionary movement and its military
leaders. Within such a movement, leadership struggles are
likely to be settled by purge, and such purges are likely to gain
a momentum that gives them lives of their own.

Because they tend to be men who are committed, and because they become habituated to the exercise of independent
judgment, the commanders of revolutionary forces are unlikely
to prove unquestioningly obedient to orders that experience
tells them are impracticable, or to be readily responsive to policies they deem seriously inconsistent with the cause for which
they believe themselves to be fighting. Such differences of perspective are likely to become exaggerated when, as is often the
case, the top command has its headquarters at a distance, perhaps in an urban center or in another country. That was so, to
cite three illustrations, in the cases of the Hukbalahap rebellion,
the early phase of the Chinese communist revolution, and the
1954–62 Algerian war of independence.

The Political Bureau of the Philippine Communist Party, its

directives disregarded by the Communist leaders of the Hukbalahap, had physically to leave its secret headquarters in downtown Manila and travel to the Huk headquarters in the Sierra
Madre in order to relieve Luis Taruc of the supreme command
and appoint José Lava, the general secretary of the Party, to take
his place.[37] Mao Zedong, while building his Red Army base in
Jiangxi Province, refused to follow military policies laid down
by the Party Center in Shanghai because he considered them
wrong, and when it ordered him to leave the Red Army and
report to the Party Center, he did not obey.[38] During the Algerian war for independence there was bitter strife between political and military leaders in Algeria and between the military
leaders and the Algerian government-in-exile in Tunisia; indeed, it took some years after independence had been won for
those leadership struggles to end.[39]

The Chinese Red Army in Jiangxi contained a pyramidal
Party structure and had over it a system of political commis-
sars, arrangements providing an alternate chain of command,
which in theory should have ensured subordination to the
Party Center. They did not because Mao Zedong was the Red
Army's top political commissar and because he dominated its
internal Party organization. The Chinese Communist Party,
like the Communist Party of the Soviet Union, had an intelligence and security apparatus intended, among other things, to
enforce obedience to the Party Center. Its arm was not long
enough, however, to reach into Jiangxi, and there Mao had a
secret police apparatus of his own. When the leaders of one of
the Red armies sided with the Party Center and against Mao
Zedong on certain matters of military and agrarian policy, Mao
employed that apparatus, to the accompaniment of vague
charges of infiltration by a secret Kuomintang organization, to
initiate a purge against them and their subordinates. When in-
terrogations are conducted under torture the list of suspects
tends to increase by geometric progression, and in this purge
some 4,400 men were arrested and between 2,000 and 3,000
lost their lives.[40] Such purges, it should be admitted, can also
occur within non-communist revolutionary movements. In the
Algerian war for independence, the commanders of three of the
six *wilayas,* or zones, bitterly at odds with the Algerian govern-

ment-in-exile and also fearful of infiltration by French agents, conducted purges more long lasting than that which took place under Mao Zedong, which were no less deadly.[41]

Mao Zedong's purge of supporters in Jiangxi of the Party Center helped to precipitate a shift of the Party's headquarters and top leadership from Shanghai to Jiangxi, a move that made it possible to curb his exercise of personal authority. In 1931 a Moscow-trained cadre named Deng Fa was brought there to establish a new political security apparatus, and in 1932 Zhou Enlai replaced Mao as top political commissar of the Red Forces. In 1934, as will be recounted in the chapter that follows, nationalist military pressure compelled the Communists to abandon Jiangxi and undertake the retreat known as the Long March. This damaged the moral authority of those who had been in charge during the immediately preceding period in which Mao had been in eclipse. In consequence, during a pause in the Long March, he succeeded in regaining the ascendancy over the Red Army that he had lost to Zhou Enlai, and the subsequent stages of that retreat found Mao enjoying the support of the political security apparatus as well.[42] He never again lost it, and in later years, headed by his former bodyguard Wang Dongxing, it became a pervasive organization, which included a security guard force of at least division size.[43]

External Aid and Foreign Control

It is frequently charged that this or that revolutionary struggle or war of resistance is under the control of an outside power. There is an element of paradox about charges of alien control where struggles against foreign domination are concerned. However, not all conflicts fall neatly into one category or another, and both revolutionary movements and wars of resistance are likely to be given outside help and encouragement. Such help and encouragement may be adduced in support of charges of foreign control, but such charges always deserve to be approached with skepticism.

The problems of the PKP headquarters in Manila with the Huks under the leadership of Taruc, of the Party Center in

Shanghai with Mao Zedong in Jiangxi, and of the Algerian government-in-exile with the six zonal commands in Algeria itself all bear witness to the fact that irregular forces and their commanders are not easily controlled by their own organizational superiors. That being so, logic suggests that it would be still more difficult for a foreign power to exercise domination over them.

The most persistent attempt by one country to control the course of another country's revolution, at least in modern times, was undoubtedly Soviet Russia's long involvement in the affairs of China. In the 1920s the Soviet Union provided military aid in the forms of arms, ammunition, advisers, and instructors to the revolutionary Kuomintang led by Chiang Kai-shek, but found that it could not control him even during the period in which he was dependent on it for essential support. As soon as he had gained access to Chinese financial resources adequate to his needs, he purged the Chinese Communists from the Kuomintang and sent his Russian advisers home. In the 30 July 1949 letter of transmittal of the China White Paper, published in the wake of the Communist takeover, Secretary of State Dean Acheson declared that the leaders of the Chinese Communist Party were "subservient to a foreign power, Russia."[44] It did appear so at the time, but after the Sino-Soviet split over a decade later, it became known that the reality had been different. At the end of World War II Stalin had advised the Chinese Communists to make their peace with Chiang Kai-shek.[45] Stalin had evidently admired Chiang Kai-shek and distrusted the Chinese Communists, and they had justified his distrust by disregarding his advice—advice that, if followed, would undoubtedly have proved fatal to their cause.

It is also instructive to note that in the years beginning with 1949, China provided a sanctuary in which Vietnam's communist insurgents could be trained and refitted. China supplied the artillery that ensured French defeat at Dien Bien Phu, and between 1965 and 1968 some fifty thousand Chinese engineering and anti-aircraft troops were stationed in North Vietnam in support of Hanoi's war effort.[46] In fact, if the Chinese Communists' account is to be accepted, they extended a total of $20 billion in aid to their Vietnamese comrades. Yet not long after those comrades had taken Saigon, they began to expel the residents of Cholon, the city's Chinese quarter, and other people of Chinese race, and in 1979 the two countries fought a border war.[47]

All this suggests that attempts by outsiders to control a country's revolution are not likely to succeed, and that the gratitude earned by foreign aid—even aid crucial to the success of a revolution or a resistance movement—can be expected to prove transitory.

In pondering the foregoing discussion of the relationship between organization and motivation, one may see the imperative of decentralization that characterizes guerrilla warfare as the key link in a chain. This imperative leads, first of all, to the need for a self-imposed discipline that can only arise from commitment to the objectives of the struggle. Since nationalism motivates so many wars of the third kind, such committed revolutionaries—while they may appreciate outside help—are unlikely to allow their movements to fall under foreign control. The participants may differ over the best means of attaining their common objective. They may also see it from quite different perspectives. Inasmuch as they have staked their lives on it, moreover, their differences are likely to be passionately held. Accordingly, these movements, and particularly revolutionary ones, are by their nature prone to factionalism and leadership struggles, with the connection between headquarters and field commands a particularly sensitive nexus. Indeed, as illustrated by the Chinese case, the need for decentralization of operations leads to horizontal, loosely structured development of the support organizations on which field forces depend, in contradistinction to the verticality of organization that characterizes conventional forces and facilitates command. Finally, in considering the dual factors of organization and motivation, one sees that motivation is the more clearly indispensable requirement for conducting wars of the third kind, while organization may lay the foundations of a post-war structure through which the movement's organization men will govern.

Guerrillas, as a general proposition, must rely upon a strategy of protracted war, hoping for a favorable outcome achieved through the intervention of an outside party, the erosion of the opponent's will to continue the struggle, or a reversal of the balance of forces between the two sides. Thus, to cite examples, the Cubans' second struggle for independence from Spain was brought to a successful conclusion at the turn of the century through the intervention of the United States; the eight-year Algerian war for independence ended in 1962 with France, though holding the upper hand militarily, drained of the will to continue the struggle; and the Chinese Communists, through the attrition they imposed on nationalist armies and the growth of their own capabilities, were able after two decades to defeat those armies and gain control of all mainland China. It is cases of this third category that are the most interesting because sufficient alteration of the balance of forces and other favorable circumstances may make it possible for guerrillas, incapable as such of winning large-scale conventional battles of position and maneuver, to be converted into an army that can.

Those other circumstances, it will be appreciated, must include the availability of sufficient matériel to support the transition from the hit-and-run operations of lightly armed forces to conventional warfare with its requirement of heavier weapons and extended periods of combat. It is at this point of conversion that the captured arms and ammunition on which guerrillas largely depend are likely to be insufficient and that access to outside sources of supply may prove crucial, as was illustrated during the 1910–20 Mexican Revolution by the respective careers of Francisco Villa and Emiliano Zapata. In 1913 Villa, a former cattle rustler and bandit chief, led two thousand irregulars in a successful night attack on the border town of Ciudad Juárez. Its capture gave Villa access to arms and ammunition from the United States, which he paid for with confiscated cattle, cotton, and bank funds, and within a year he had an army of forty thousand.[1] The peasant leader Zapata was based in the land-locked state of Morelos, south of Mexico City, and had to get any weapons heavier than rifles and the bulk of his ammunition by capture from federal garrisons. In 1913 he succeeded in creating a semi-regular army, but it took upward of 200,000 rounds of ammunition for a force of three to four thousand of his men to besiege a town for five days, and this made it difficult for him to sustain the rhythm essential to successful conventional operations. Loosely allied with Villa, Zapata twice succeeded in entering Mexico City, but possession of it proved indecisive. On one of those occasions he might have pushed down the rail line to the port of Vera Cruz, which would have given him access to foreign sources of supply and denied them to the opposing forces of Venustiano Carranza, but failed to do so.[2] In consequence the major battles that followed were between Carrancistas and Villistas; Villa was defeated, and Zapata had to retire to Morelos and resume his dependence on guerrilla operations.

In Indochina access to outside sources of arms and ammunition enabled the Communist Viet Minh to convert the guerrilla forces they had begun building during World War II into the regular army that forced France to abandon Indochina in 1954. They had obtained some arms for their guerrilla forces from the defeated Japanese and got more by purchase from Chinese Nationalists who came to accept the Japanese surrender. The first French divisions arrived only in 1946, and by the latter part of 1947 Viet Minh guerrillas had made large areas impervious to French thrusts. But it was only after victorious Chinese communist armies arrived at the border in November 1949 that the Viet Minh could receive the logistic support needed to convert guerrilla forces into regularly organized battalions. A year later they had captured all the French posts along the border, and soon thereafter the Viet Minh order of battle contained first regiments and then divisional forces. In January 1951 they were ready to begin the offensive operations that culminated in the May 1954 surrender of the French fortress complex at Dien Bien Phu and the cease-fire of 20 July 1954.

The penalty for abandoning the hit-and-run war of the guerrilla for large-scale battles of position and maneuver before having achieved a favorable balance of forces can be a serious defeat and the need to revert to guerrilla warfare at a reduced level. That was the case early in 1968 in South Vietnam, where some eighty thousand Viet Cong carried out synchronized attacks on all the country's major cities, thirty-six of forty-four provincial capitals, and scores of district towns.[3] This nationwide offensive was launched in the expectation of touching off urban uprisings as well as of causing a collapse of the Army of the Republic of Vietnam (ARVN), and the teams of infiltrating Viet Cong, after seizing their respective objectives in surprise night attacks, were to hold them until main force troops moved in. The urban uprisings did not occur, however, the ARVN did not collapse, and a last-minute redeployment of U.S. units prevented communist main forces from entering Saigon. In that city and nearby places, Viet Cong teams totaling in the low thousands attacked the U.S. embassy, the presidential palace, the headquarters of General William C. Westmorland, South Vietnamese general staff offices, the main radio station, and other objectives. The attacks on some of these objectives were frustrated, but the Viet Cong who seized others held out for as long as three weeks against greatly superior U.S. and ARVN forces.[4] In this offensive, which took its name from the Vietnamese lunar New Year, known as Tet, the South Vietnamese Communists lost many political cadres who came into the open for the purpose of leading the expected uprising, as well as many of the Viet Cong.[5]

General Tran Van Tra, communist commander for the lower half of South Vietnam, in which Saigon is situated, wrote later

that the Communists' error was to have failed to correctly estimate the balance of forces between the two sides.[6] (That was
also true on the American side: thus, on 15 November 1967,
while in Washington on consultation, General Westmoreland
publicly asserted that the ranks of the Viet Cong were steadily
thinning, and that the important point had been reached where
an end to the war had begun to come into view.)[7] In reaction to
the failure of its Tet offensive, the communist Central Office
for South Vietnam—the Lao Dong (Communist Party) regional headquarters—adopted a resolution that recognized the
need for the Viet Cong to fall back on a war of small-unit
operations.[8]

The classic transformation of guerrilla forces into a conventional army, that accomplished by the Chinese Communists in
the years immediately following World War II, was the culmi-
nation of earlier attempts to create armed forces capable of successfully conducting major battles of position and maneuver.
These attempts, first in Jiangxi between 1927 and 1934 and later
in North China during World War II, were premature and led
to defeats, but provided lessons on which final success was
built.

During the first three years of its existence, the Red Army,
based in southern Jiangxi, with Zhu De as its top commander
and Mao Zedong as its political commissar, defeated three attacks launched against it by provincial troops. In consequence
of these victories, and in part by recruiting captured soldiers,
the Red Army soon grew to a strength of seven thousand men.
In 1930 the top leaders of the Chinese Communist Party, then
based in Shanghai, ordered the Red Army, as well as other
communist forces conducting guerrilla operations in neighboring provinces, to be regularized in preparation for attacks on
Nanchang and Changsha, capitals respectively of Jiangxi and
Hunan, as well as on Wuhan, the tricity center of Hubei province. Writing to Party headquarters, Mao resisted these orders,
objecting that the tactics through which the Red Army had
gained its successes were those of guerrilla warfare, but his objections were overruled. The attacks on the cities were to have
been the signal for uprisings by communist-organized workers, but they failed to take place. One corps of the reorganized

Red Army took Changsha, but was driven out after a few days; Nanchang resisted all efforts to take it; the forces advancing on Wuhan never got within striking distance of that center; and still another force, marching up from the southern province of Guangxi, suffered heavy losses on the way and arrived too late to take part in the fighting. It had by then become obvious to the forces operating against Nanchang and Changsha that they were not up to the task of conducting positional warfare against major centers, and at Mao's urging they returned to their base.[9] But Chiang Kai-shek had now been alerted to the potential danger of the communist forces, and henceforth they would have to do battle not merely with provincial troops but with nationalist government armies.

Between 1930 and 1934 Chiang launched five successive campaigns against the Communists' Jiangxi base. The defense against the first three of these campaigns, which the Communists conducted in accordance with Mao's precepts, depended upon deliberately induced penetration of the communist base by enemy forces as a prelude to their entrapment. In the third of these campaigns, with the Communists enforcing scorched earth practices and the evacuation of villages along the route on which the enemy was advancing, the Nationalists found themselves reduced to harvesting and eating unripe grain and drinking foul water. Finally, wearied by fruitless marching and with many of their men sick, the Nationalists were caught in a series of large-scale ambushes. The communist accomplishment in this campaign, an American military historian has observed, represented "people's war" at its best.[10]

Ironically, the success of the strategy employed in that campaign helped lead the Communists to abandon it. They had extended their base area into western Fujian, approximately doubling its size, and acquired many modern weapons by capture. With a regular army of seventy thousand, in addition to lesser units, they were now determined to conduct the defense of their base beyond its borders.[11] That they were able to frustrate Chiang Kai-shek's fourth campaign was owing in part to their success in breaking the military codes of the Nationalists and devising battle plans based on knowledge of the latter's intended movements.[12] However, Chiang conducted his fifth anticommunist offensive, begun in October 1933, in accordance with a strategy of blockade and siege that prevented the Communists from employing mobile operations. Not ready for positional warfare against the better-armed nationalist armies, and continually losing ground, in October 1934 the Communists broke out of what remained of their base and began the year-long retreat known as the Long March to the Yenan area of northwestern China.[13]

The outbreak of the 1937–45 war with Japan found the Chinese Communists installed in their new base around Yenan with a three-division Red Army of some thirty thousand troops, which the government gave the new designation of the Eighth Route Army. At Mao's insistence it did not begin its operations as a unit. Instead, its three divisions crossed the Yellow River into Shanxi province separately and dispersed into units that engaged in mobilizing popular support and troop recruitment. Having grown to appropriate size, each unit was intended to subdivide, amoebalike, into units that were to repeat the process. By the summer of 1940 the growth of the three divisions was such that they were able to contribute a total of 115 regiments—some four hundred thousand troops—to the so-called Hundred Regiments Campaign in wide areas of North China. The 115 regiments were assisted by a militia numbering one hundred thousand, led by hundreds of young graduates of the Communists' Resistance University, who were responsible for pre-positioning food, ammunition, and supplies; for removing steel rails and ties in order to hamper the enemy's transport; for harassing Japanese reinforcements; and for evacuating the wounded.[14] On 20 August 1940 the participating regiments went on the offensive simultaneously in five provinces of North China. In a first phase that lasted three weeks, the primary objectives were rail lines. This was followed by a second and slightly shorter phase in which attacks were made on Japanese strong points and on blockhouses that had been advanced into guerrilla territory. In a third period of two-month duration, the Japanese regrouped their forces and launched widespread counteroffensive operations, which the Communists fiercely resisted.[15]

In the wake of the Hundred Regiments Campaign, the Japanese adopted a *Sankō-seisaku* or "three-all" policy, which called for conducting operations in communist base areas during which they would "kill all, burn all and destroy all." At first communist forces fought pitched battles in defense of villages under attack and to prevent the destruction of crops, but the cost proved unacceptably high.[16] Accordingly, in December 1941 the Central Committee of the Chinese Communist Party issued a directive calling for the dispersal of elements of the Eighth Route Army into units of squad and platoon size, and for concentration on guerrilla warfare.[17] The "three-all" campaign had done enormous damage to the Communists' human and material support base. It had resulted in the deaths of thousands of young cadres, reduced Eighth Route Army strength by one-quarter, forced the Communists to withdraw from wide areas, and reduced the population under their control from forty-five million to under thirty million. However, that campaign has also been credited with driving the peasantry and the Eighth Route Army into a closer alliance and making the communist revolution irreversible.[18]

In the two years following the decision to concentrate on guerrilla warfare, the officers and men of the Eighth Route Army are said to have conducted some 32,000 small-unit operations. Dispersed as they were in villages of the North China countryside, they also accomplished a great expansion of militia forces.[19] Meanwhile, American pressure on the Japanese in the Pacific was impelling them to transfer eight full divisions from North China. In the wake of this partial Japanese withdrawal, the Eighth Route Army began to reconcentrate forces for the renewal of conflict with the Nationalists expected to follow the anticipated defeat of Japan.[20]

In the spring of 1945 the Chinese Communists, by their own account, had an army of 910,000 regulars and 2,200,000 militia, though the Americans credited them with but 600,000 regulars and a militia of 400,000. At about that same time, the Chinese government had an army of 3,000,000, including thirty-nine U.S.-equipped divisions, and an air force in the process of being built to a strength of eight and one-third groups. Thus the government had an estimated five-to-one superiority in combat troops, a practical monopoly of heavy weapons and equipment, and an air force that was unopposed.[21]

On 14 August 1945, the day of Japan's surrender, an order was issued by General Douglas MacArthur, as supreme commander of the Allied Powers, designating the national government of China as the entity to which Japanese forces in the China theater were to surrender.[22] In order to help that government reoccupy Japanese-held areas and take the surrender of Japanese troops, U.S. forces transported three nationalist armies by air to key parts of East and North China and sealifted others until between 400,000 and 500,000 had been moved to new positions.[23] In consequence of these arrangements the Communists were prevented from acquiring arms and ammunition from surrendering Japanese troops. Thus it was the Nationalists who were able to take the surrender of the great majority of the 1,200,000 Japanese troops stationed in what was then referred to as China proper, and to acquire their equipment and stocks of matériel.[24]

However, in Manchuria, which had been under Japanese control since 1931 and had been overrun by Soviet Russian forces in the final days of World War II, the Communists were more fortunate. The forces they sent to Manchuria, from which the Russians were soon to withdraw, arrived well ahead of the Nationalists and were allowed to take over arms and equipment surrendered by some 700,000 Japanese and puppet troops. The acquisition of these stocks undoubtedly played a major role in determining the course of the struggle for Manchuria that ensued, but because the decisive campaign of the civil war had begun in intramural China before the communist conquest of Manchuria had been completed, the stocks no longer needed in that region could not be shipped south of the Great Wall in time to help decide the outcome there.[25]

In North China, with the outbreak of renewed civil war, the nationalist strategy resembled that of the Japanese, whose place the Nationalists had taken. It depended on urban centers and transport lines, while the strategy of the Communists rested on control of the populace of the surrounding countryside. In the event, the communist forces—now called the People's Liberation Army—proved able to capture and stockpile the kinds and quantities of weapons and matériel needed to conduct a war of position and maneuver, and to win the climactic campaign of the Chinese civil war, the Huai-Hai campaign, which took its name from geographic features of the southern part of the North China Plain where it was fought.

During the Huai-Hai campaign, which pitted against each other two great armies each numbering about a half million men, the nationalist armies were supported by a conventional logistic system operating in an area containing a relatively well-developed transport net. The communist forces were served by a logistic system, primitive in its material equipment, that operated under the direction of an ad hoc "front committee" of the Party headed by Deng Xiaoping. Two main communist armies had been combined for the campaign, and in preparation for it, the front committee could draw on not only the political workers of the armies but also on the political cadres of the North China, Central China, and East China regional bureaus of the Party. Under their direction, guerrillas harassed the nationalist forces, while the organized populace of the countryside was mobilized for the digging of trenches and construction of fortifications; the assembly, pre-positioning and final movement by porters of the supplies needed to feed the troops and maintain ammunition levels; the evacuation of the wounded; and the replacement of combat losses. The dispersed nature of this logistic system tended to minimize the advantages accruing to the Nationalists from their undisputed command of the air, as did the habitual recourse of communist troops to movement by night.[26]

In the actual campaign, which began on 7 November 1948, the pervasive and dependable nature of the Communists' logistic system—more than two million peasants pushed their wheelbarrowloads of ammunition, food, and fuel around the battlefields—gave the communist troops extraordinary freedom of movement. The Nationalists were held in what became a dangerous salient—apparently on orders from Chiang Kai-shek, who tried to direct operations from Defense Ministry headquarters in Nanjing. In consequence the Communists were able to surround three nationalist armies, after which they succeeded in blocking and destroying a fourth that had been advancing toward the battle zone to their rescue. Meanwhile, the surrounded armies, inadequately supplied by airdrop with food for the men and fuel for the tanks, had been trying in vain to break out. On 20 December bad weather closed in that did not lift, permitting the resumption of airdrops, until 29 December. The final communist general offensive, against 130,000 surviving nationalist troops who had been squeezed into a small perimeter, was launched on 6 January 1949, and by 10 January all coordinated resistance was over. The campaign cost the Nationalists some 400,000 men, and they had now lost the last of their U.S.-equipped divisions. It was followed five days later by their abandonment of the defense works remaining between the battlefield and the Yangzi River. Now nothing but that river lay between the communist armies and the nationalist capital of Nanjing.

In the region to the south of the Yangzi into which they next moved, however, the Communists had no organized basis of popular support. Accordingly, the logistics of the People's Liberation Army, like those of other regular armies, would depend upon the control of urban centers and of main transport lines.

In reflecting on the foregoing it might be observed that there was a parallel between the Hundred Regiments Campaign of the Eighth Route Army and the Viet Cong's Tet offensive. Both were far-flung operations, each was conducted in the context of a highly unfavorable balance of forces, and both resulted in military setbacks requiring reversion to small-scale guerrilla operations. The success of the Chinese Communists in the climactic Huai-Hai campaign of position and maneuver had as a partial parallel the decisive Viet Minh victory over the French in the positional battle at Dien Bien Phu, but was more impressive for having been won without access to outside sources of supply. Indeed, though it is common for guerrillas to meet most of their needs by capture, it is quite another thing—as testified by Zapata's logistic problems during the Mexican Revolution—to capture and accumulate the kinds and quantities of arms and supplies needed for conventional operations. Finally, it was perhaps one of the misfortunes of the Chinese Nationalists to enjoy the logistic support of the United States and have on hand everything that a Japanese army of 1,200,000 men and its Chinese puppet auxiliaries had surrendered at the end of World War II. Had the Nationalists been less well supplied, they might have taken better care not to lose so much of what they had to the Communists.

5 Conceptual Approaches to Counterinsurgency

There are, it must be appreciated, important differences between armed resistance to a foreign foe on the soil of one's country and armed opposition to domestic authority. Nevertheless, it is common practice to depict those who take up arms against us as being in rebellion against authority, and *counterinsurgency,* with its connotation of rebellion, is the only commonly recognized word that can be used to designate the range of measures that have as their aim the suppression of those who have taken up arms against either foreign intrusion or internal authority. *Counterguerrilla operations* would be preferable, being free of the taint of euphemism, but it suggests a narrower focus. Accordingly, we may use the word *counterinsurgency* when the context does not require us to distinguish between the two main categories of wars of the third kind.

In the two immediately preceding chapters we considered the organizational aspects of insurgency, the development of guerrilla forces, and the transformation of such forces into armies capable of successfully conducting wars of position and maneuver. In their writings on protracted war, Mao Zedong in China and Vietnam's General Vo Nguyen Giap describe such war as having three phases, and Western analysts, without adhering closely to either of their formulations, have identified the first stage as that of organization and preparation; the second as that of guerrilla warfare; and the third as that of conventional warfare.[1]

As will be apparent from the preceding chapters, the three phases cannot in actual practice be sharply distinguished from one another. In the case of the Chinese Communists, organizational work was initiated in difficult and mountainous terrain and extended outward from there to more settled areas by armed units that already had a guerrilla capability. Moreover, the organizational work of the first period was carried over into a long period of active guerrilla and mobile operations, and guerrilla operations did not end with the initiation by main force units of a war of position and maneuver. Accordingly, the transition from one phase of an insurgency to another can be seen as representing an accretion of capabilities accompanying quantitative growth. It should also be recalled that a premature transition to a war of position and maneuver will compel insurgents to drop back to the lower stage of guerrilla warfare, whereas—inasmuch as our concern is not with conventional military operations—a successful transition marks the end of our interest.

Organization alone, as observed, is not enough to provide the basis for a successful insurgency: there must also be a cause to which the populace, or at least a substantial part of it, can be expected to respond. Accordingly, a government's problem in dealing with the pre-guerrilla phase of an insurgency is the political and administrative one of providing governance that deals with the sources of popular dissatisfaction and an application of police power against those engaged in terrorist or other illegal acts in promoting the insurgency.

It is in the second, or guerrilla, phase of an insurgency that government forces will be introduced into the equation and that the conceptual approach that guides them becomes crucially important. Counterinsurgency operations may have as their direct target the guerrillas themselves, or they may be aimed variously at the noncombatants who support them, the material means by which their logistic needs are met, or their organizational infrastructure. In addition, the approach may variously be one that treats members of the populace who support the guerrillas as enemies; that takes no particular interest

in the nature of the impact of counterguerrilla operations upon
the populace amidst which they are conducted; or that regards
the protection of the people and enlisting their loyalty as vital
to the success of the counterinsurgency. Finally, it will be found
in practice that counterinsurgency operations generally involve
a mix of means, and that what matters most is where the main
emphasis is placed.

In 1962 President John F. Kennedy expressed the belief that
dealing with insurgency would require "a whole new kind of
strategy, a wholly different kind of force, and therefore a new
and wholly different kind of military training." In reaction to
this thesis, General George H. Decker, the army chief of staff,
declared that "any good soldier can handle guerrillas."[2] Whatever the merits of that evaluation insofar as the respective tactical
abilities of soldiers and guerrillas are concerned, it represented a
conventional approach to the problems of unconventional warfare. The approach of General Harold K. Johnson, who succeeded General Decker at a time when large numbers of American combat troops were about to be introduced into Vietnam,
was similarly conventional. The means of providing stability in
South Vietnam, he asserted, consisted in finding the enemy,
fixing him where he could be engaged successfully, and then
fighting and finishing him off.[3] It is not apparent that either
General Decker or General Johnson took into account the difficulty of finding and fixing in place guerrillas, whose basic requirements are best met through dispersion amidst the rural
populace that provides them with logistic and other support
and who need not concentrate in the defense of any particular
center of population because none are vital to them.

The Conventional Approach in Practice: Places as Objectives

Pondering his experience as a partisan leader during World War
I, T. E. Lawrence wrote that most wars are wars of contact,
with forces striving to keep in touch with the object of avoiding tactical surprise, but that irregular forces should conduct a
war of detachment, as befits those who depend on surprise.[4]
Henry Halleck, one of the founders of American strategic stud-

ies, defined strategy as the art of directing masses at decisive points—a concept reflected in the practice of selecting military objectives in terms of taking particular places, but not pertinent when there are no decisive points.[5]

During the Philippine Insurrection, to cite one example of the misapplication of the principle Halleck set forth, American troops occupied and abandoned a place named Porac so many times that they used to say, "When there isn't anything else to do, we go out and take Porac before breakfast."[6] With guerrillas slipping away each time in advance of an attack, such operations run the risks of creating frustration on the part of troops and antagonism among local people, especially when supposed guerrilla positions are "softened up" with artillery fire before the troops move in.

A more recent example of a conventional approach to unconventional warfare, in that same context of places as objectives, was provided during the Vietnam War by General Paul D. Harkins during his tour as commander, U.S. Military Assistance Command, Vietnam (MACV). In January 1963 units of the Army of the Republic of Vietnam (ARVN) had a pitched battle with a battalion of Viet Cong near the village of Ap Bac. In this encounter the ARVN deployed one battalion of regulars, two battalions of civil guards, and a company of armored personnel carriers, together with artillery and air support. During the day of the battle the Viet Cong shot down five helicopters and inflicted almost two hundred casualties, and after night had fallen they slipped away undetected. General Harkins reported Ap Bac as a victory for the ARVN because it had "taken the objective."[7]

The Conventional Approach: Search-and-Destroy Operations

Search-and-destroy operations have been described as operations conducted for the purpose of seeking out and destroying enemy forces, installations, resources, and base areas, and as such they represent the application of a strategy of attrition. Most often these operations have as their principal objective the enemy forces themselves, and it is common for the troops engaged in them to cordon off areas that are then combed in an effort to flush out enemy forces. In the Philippines, during World War II, sweeping operations by tough Japanese troops inflicted heavy casualties on newly formed Hukbalahap guerrilla forces, but with experience the Huks learned to survive similar operations in the same areas with minimal casualties.[8]

Because military sweeps are necessarily conducted by forces of substantial size, they can hardly be expected to achieve surprise, and even large bodies of troops find it difficult to cordon off large areas tightly enough to prevent many guerrillas from slipping through or to comb them thoroughly enough to catch a high proportion of those who remain in hiding. And because sweeps are never more than partially successful, they are almost certain to be repeated, with civilians suffering at the hands of frustrated soldiers and made enemies thereby. In the Algerian resistance of 1954–62, for example, the French carried out sweeps during which selected zones were bombed and in which tanks were used to destroy villages—operations called *ratissages,* or "rakings." From the standpoint of the Algerian rebels these operations were not an unmixed evil: the *ratissages,* one of their leaders asserted, were their "best recruiting agent."[9]

The seriousness of the problem of achieving surprise in operations of this sort may be gauged from experience in Vietnam: fewer than 1 percent of even small-unit operations conducted by the ARVN resulted in contact with the enemy, and the great majority of all battles were at the time, place, and duration of their enemy's choice.[10] In consequence of enemy ability to give or avoid battle almost at will, ARVN and U.S. forces were unable to impose on enemy forces more losses than the latter were able to replace. Thus failure to reach what was called "the cross-over point" meant the failure of the ARVN and U.S. strategy of attrition.[11]

The ability of the Viet Cong to replace losses was a reflection of the wide measure of political success they had achieved among the people of the countryside and of their ability to rely on the three-level military system described earlier in connection with the Chinese People's Liberation Army. In such cases replacements of casualties among full-time fighters will be drawn from local self-defense units, and in protracted war, new recruits will continually be coming of the age to bear arms. In consequence of this regenerative capacity, many casualties may be suffered without resulting in a comparable reduction in the size of a guerrilla army.

Even so, American officers found the failure of the strategy of attrition as the United States applied it in Vietnam—where the total munitions expended were greater than the tonnage the United States used worldwide during World War II—to be a baffling experience.[12] On 27 November 1964, while briefing Washington officials on the situation in Vietnam, General Maxwell D. Taylor had the following to say:

> The ability of the Viet Cong continuously to rebuild their units and to make good their losses is one of the mysteries of this guerrilla war. We are aware of the recruiting methods by which local boys are induced or compelled to join the Viet Cong ranks and have some general appreciation of the amount of infiltration of personnel from outside. Yet taking both of these sources into account, we still find no plausible explanation of the continued strength of the Viet Cong if our data on Viet Cong losses are even approximately correct.[13]

Policies of Reconcentration, Resettlement, Depopulation, and Devastation

"As often as not," Admiral Stansfield Turner has observed, "wars are won or lost on the question of supplies." In consequence, logistics usually dominate strategy.[14] Guerrillas may vanish upon the approach of a superior enemy, but their main source of logistic and other support is a populace that must stay in place. As a British officer of the colonial era observed: "The hostile bands may elude regular detachments, but their villages and flocks remain."[15] It is observations of this sort that suggested a strategy of indirection under which the perhaps scattered populace of a countryside that harbors guerrillas is either relocated within it, in settlements where it can be more readily controlled, or is removed from it entirely. In the latter case, abandoned homes, livestock, orchards, and crops may be systematically destroyed, evacuated areas treated as free fire zones, and people encountered there liable to suffer the treatment accorded guerrillas.

In South Vietnam, beginning under Ngo Dinh Diem, peasants were uprooted from their native villages and reconcentrated in new settlements initially called *agrovilles,* and later strategic hamlets. The strategic hamlets had defense works, and the inhabitants were intended to defend them against entry by the Viet Cong, who were thereby to be deprived of peasant support. But the inhabitants of the strategic hamlets by and large resented being made to leave their native villages, were disenchanted with the Diem regime on other grounds as well, and saw little reason to risk their lives by opposing the Viet Cong. In this and other respects, the planning of the program and its implementation were defective, and the resources and effort devoted to it were worse than wasted.[16]

In Manchuria, beginning in 1932, the invading Japanese reconcentrated the peasantry in new villages, which they kept under tight control. The farm buildings from which the peasants and their belongings had been removed were destroyed in order to deprive Chinese guerrillas of shelter and hiding places, both important because much of Manchuria is a treeless plain and the winters are so cold that people cannot survive in the open.[17] Manchuria's mountainous and forested areas, although providing hiding places and cover, lacked the sources of logistic support and recruits that guerrilla forces require if they are to flourish, and those who did not give up crossed the border into the USSR, only returning with the Soviet forces that overran Manchuria in the closing days of World War II.[18]

More common than reconcentrating the people of rural areas in newly constructed villages and allowing them to continue with their agricultural pursuits has been the practice of compelling them to leave the land for urban centers or refugee camps and then devastating the countryside from which resistance forces had been drawing their support. Such provision as has been made in these cases for the housing and sustaining of the people evacuated from the countryside—always a consideration secondary to the pursuit of military operations—has in practice left them in wretched circumstances, and in some cases no such provision has been made at all.

In 1896, during Cuba's war of independence, General Weyler—having promised that he would bring all resistance to Spanish authority to an end within thirty days—had some four hundred thousand people removed from rural areas to garrison towns. There they remained while the rebellion continued, and in the two years that followed thousands died of starvation, exposure, and disease. Next door, in the United States, accounts of the suffering of the *reconcentrados* aroused popular concern and helped bring on the Spanish-American War. It is thus ironic that Americans used the same strategy of reconcentration accompanied by devastation in asserting their authority over the Philippines, acquired from Spain as part of the peace settlement. On the island of Samar, which was ordered turned into a "howling wilderness," general deprivation led to widespread lawlessness, which continued long after all genuine insurgents had been killed or had laid down their arms.[19] In Batangas province the devastation carried out was so nearly complete that the people held at reconcentration centers could not all be fed, and it took years for the losses in population and agricultural production to be made good.[20]

Less common than the practice of reconcentrating the populations of rural areas, but more ruthless, has been recourse to efforts to depopulate them entirely. We have already described the Japanese attempt to depopulate and devastate parts of North China during World War II, and a similar episode marked the presidency in Mexico of General Victoriano Huerta, undoubtedly the most sinister figure to appear on the stage during the Mexican Revolution. In April 1913, before a gathering in Mexico City of the principal *hacendados* of the state of Morelos, where the planting season was at hand, but the peasants were in rebellion, Huerta promised to restore peace in the state within a period of one month. He intended to do this, he said, by depopulating the state and sending in other workers for its haciendas. In order to supply the needed workers, Huerta proposed to import thirty thousand Japanese (this sounds odd now, but it was a period during which thousands of Japanese were being shipped to Brazil and Peru as plantation workers).[21] General Juvencio Robles, the army commander in Morelos, ordered the rural populace reconcentrated in urban centers, with summary execution the penalty for unauthorized presence in the countryside. Thereafter, each week hundreds of farmers and field hands were taken from the reconcentration centers and shipped off in cattle cars as conscripts or for agricultural labor in other states, with their dependents left to shift for themselves. A start had been made toward depopulating the state, but soon people began fleeing to the hills upon the approach of federal troops. Huerta's harsh methods, rather than bringing the rebellion to an early end, served rather to intensify it. And the only Japanese who seem to have come were ten men employed on one hacienda as guards.[22]

Clear and Hold: The Strategy of Siege

In 1828, in a memoir for Nicholas I concerning the intended Russian conquest of the Caucasus, General Aleksei Veliaminov likened that mountainous and forested region to a mighty fortress that only thoughtless men would try to escalade. The Caucasus could be taken by siege, he said, but that might take as long as thirty years, and he accordingly suggested that other means be tried. In the event, the other measures he had in mind did not succeed, and the conquest of the Caucasus did take over thirty years, with the Russians finally falling back on the strategy of siege. The region as a whole was too vast to be besieged, but in parts of Dagestan and Tchetchnia the Russians proceeded methodically, building bridges across the chasms and attacking the beech forests with dynamite and axe. The men so engaged were protected by whole regiments of artillery. The defending forces of Imam Shamyl, with their lighter weapons, could not get within fighting distance, and in 1859 they were forced to surrender.[23]

In south-central China, between 1930 and 1933, Chiang Kai-shek conducted four successive "extermination campaigns" against the main base of the Chinese Communists. It comprised an area roughly the size of Belgium, much of it mountainous and forested, with a population of five or six million and defended by 150,000 troops. The Communists defeated all four offensives, for the most part allowing enemy divisions to penetrate deep into the area's rugged terrain and then striking one after another in ambush-style attacks. For a fifth campaign, planned under the direction of German military advisers, Chiang mobilized 800,000 men, supported by artillery and aircraft, and adopted a strategy of siege.

North of the communist-held area was a wide stretch of flat country, which the Nationalists converted into a glacis by moving out whole villages of peasant farmers, whom they resettled elsewhere, and destroying the buildings left behind. With the land drained of its people and all structures that might have provided shelter and hiding places removed, the Communists could no longer infiltrate to gather intelligence about incoming nationalist forces or to conduct guerrilla operations. Facing the communist area the Nationalists constructed and manned an east-west line of blockhouses and built connecting roads. The encirclement was completed with less elaborate lines on the other three sides, where they ran through mountainous terrain that would have made the construction of blockhouses with connecting roads very difficult.[24]

Instead of sending their troop columns into the Communists' base, where they might have been trapped as before, the Nationalists advanced the east-west blockade line southward under cover of artillery fire that the Communists could not match and that kept them from coming within fighting distance. A year of economic blockade and of constricting military pressure, which inflicted many casualties and reduced the communist base to a fraction of its former area, convinced the Communists that to remain was to be destroyed. In October 1934 they abandoned their base, moving out through the loosely held lines to the southwest, and began the 6,000-mile retreat of the Long March.[25]

Clear and Hold: The Outward Blockade

A strategy of blockade, but facing outward rather than inward as employed by Chiang Kai-shek in his 1933–34 anticommunist campaign, was used by the British in South Africa during the 1899–1902 Boer War. As a conventional force logistically dependent on rail transport, the British army built lines of fortified posts and high tensile wire to protect the railways against guerrilla attacks. Sir Alfred Milner, the British high commissioner, had advocated a policy of establishing protected areas, centered on towns and progressively extended outward into countryside cleared of guerrillas, after which there was to be a restoration of civilian life. This clear-and-hold strategy had at first not appealed to Lord Kitchener, the British military commander, perhaps because he was only too well aware that after having been cleared from an area, guerrillas have a way of coming back in. However, it occurred to him that the lines of wire and fortified posts could be turned to offensive purposes by building additional lines outward from them to create cages into which guerrillas might be driven and trapped. In addition, in keeping with the strategy Milner had suggested, Kitchener had the ends closed, after the areas had been cleared of guerrillas, with similar blockade lines. Kitchener's drives across the veld and toward the cages, initiated during the last months of the war, swept in numbers of cattle but failed to bag many guerrillas, for most of them moved away into difficult terrain to which the system could not be readily extended. However, several thousand square miles had been cleared of guerrillas and established as protected areas.[26]

On the North China Plain during World War II the Japanese, adapting the same methods to their own requirements, dug deep ditches and built blockhouses along the line of the north-south Peking-Hankow railway, constructed cages outward from the line, and enclosed areas they had cleared. By these means they achieved a considerable measure of success, notwithstanding the digging by the Chinese of hundreds of miles of secret tunnels through which they could pass from village to village, and that served their guerrillas as hiding places. (These tunnels were the precursors of others dug by the Viet Cong in South Vietnam, which contained firing posts, aid stations, sleeping quarters, and storage facilities; as early as 1965 they were already 125 miles long.) The defense of an area of such

great length and shallow width posed enormous manpower requirements, and it ceased to be as effective as before when the
needs of other theaters led to a thinning out of Japanese forces
and to greater dependence on unreliable Chinese puppet troops.
Moreover, it was not suitable for application to the mountainous terrain west of the Peking-Hankow railway, which
skirted the edge of the North China Plain.[27]

Clear and Hold: Enclaves and the "Oil Spot" Concept

The clearing part of a clear-and-hold operation may resemble a
military sweep; it is the hold aspect that marks the important
difference between the two. The repeating of sweeping operations in response to the return of guerrillas to areas in which
troops have already conducted operations and from which they
have subsequently withdrawn, besides being wasteful of military manpower and matériel, imposes needless casualties on civilians and damage to their property. The repetition also invites
feelings of frustration among troops and raises a presumption
among civilians that the forces conducting these operations are
not up to their task of dealing with the guerrillas. By staying in
such an area in adequate numbers after it has been cleared and
conducting such operations as may be needed to prevent further guerrilla incursions, counterinsurgency forces can make
possible the restoration there of government authority.

In two cases cited above, the configuration of the area enclosed by outward-facing lines was dictated by the primary
purpose of defending railways, but operations aimed at protecting or controlling a populace may be based upon a more or less
circular shape, as one that presents the least perimeter to be defended for the area it encloses. Security within such an enclave
is provided primarily by forces operating around and beyond
its circumference, which they continually try to extend—much
as a drop of oil spreads outward when dropped on water.

The U.S. marines in Vietnam, in the beginning only a few
battalions, but finally totalling over eighty thousand, were
under the command of Major General Lewis W. Walt, who

subsequently wrote, "Soon after I arrived in Vietnam it became obvious to me that I had neither a real understanding of the nature of the war nor any clear idea of how to win it." [28] Nevertheless, he quickly realized that the people represented the key to both guerrilla and counterinsurgency operations. Under him, instead of going about by helicopter, the marines traveled on the same roads the people used and kept them open. In addition, marines were deployed in hamlets in order to keep the Viet Cong out. There they brought village militia under their wing, forming combined platoons of marines and militiamen that conducted night patrols and ambushes. The first marines had landed in the spring of 1965, and by the end of 1967 there were seventy-nine of these platoons. Each was responsible for guarding a village consisting, on the average, of five hamlets containing 3,500 people, yet only one of the platoons was ever overrun. [29]

General Westmoreland disapproved of the use of combined platoons, observing in his memoirs that they were "assiduously [sic] combing the countryside within the beachheads, trying to establish firm control in hamlets and villages, and planning to extend the beachhead gradually up and down the coast. . . . I believed the marines should have been trying to find the enemy's main forces and bring them to battle." [30] Westmoreland soon made his wishes in the matter known, many of the marine units were assigned to the operations he wanted conducted, and the marines' clear-and-hold operations remained limited. [31]

In 1968, as chairman of the Joint Chiefs of Staff, General Earle G. Wheeler seconded Westmoreland's objections to the concept of operations the marines had introduced in 1965 and rejected proposals under which Westmoreland would have been instructed that his mission was that of providing security to coastal areas, Saigon, and the Mekong delta, where the great majority of the people lived, rather than waging a war of attrition through big-unit search-and-destroy missions conducted in largely unpopulated parts of the country. These proposals had been advanced by Assistant Secretary of Defense Paul C. Warnke and other civilians in the Department of Defense. Wheeler, appalled by what he saw as an attempt to repudiate military policy, condemned the proposals and likened them to the "defensive 'enclave strategy' that some had advanced in 1966." [32] Referring to this episode in his memoirs, General Westmoreland asked: "What special audacity prompted civilian bureaucrats to deem they knew better how to run a military campaign than did military professionals?" [33] Actually, in asking for a change from reliance on attrition, they would have been in good military company—that, for example, of Lieutenant General Dave R. Palmer. When an instructor at West Point, Palmer wrote that attrition is not a strategy, but the absence of any strategy, and that the commander who resorts to it admits his failure to conceive an alternative. [34]

Problems of Intelligence: The Infrastructure and Other Targets

It should go without saying that in wars of the third kind, as in conventional wars, each side tries to get information about the enemy and tries to keep the enemy from getting information about itself. Those engaged in counterinsurgency will seek intelligence concerning the insurgents' political leaders; their military command; the size, organization, and leadership of their forces in the field; their sources of logistic and other support; and their operational plans and intentions.

Counterinsurgency forces are at a relative disadvantage in obtaining such information and putting it to effectual use, and not only because of the anonymity that civilian dress and the ability to merge into the populace give the guerrilla. I have already quoted an officer of Napoleon's army in Spain on the role of intelligence in facilitating guerrilla interdiction of French use of the roads. "Since all the inhabitants served as spies to their fellow citizens," he wrote, "the date of departure and the strength of escorts was known. Thus the bands could join together to be at least twice the enemy number." [35] Another of Napoleon's officers later recalled: "All the gold of Mexico could not have procured reliable information for the French; what was given was but a lure to make them fall more readily into snares." [36] Napoleon's armies lost half a million men in Spain, but during seven years there they never succeeded in engaging the guerrillas in pitched battle. In this situation the French, mad with frustration, committed atrocities such as those Goya depicted in the series of etchings titled *Desastres de la guerra.*

All in all, the search in the field of intelligence for a key to successful counterinsurgency operations can be as frustrating as guerrillas are elusive. Moreover, prospective sources of intelligence are commonly unwilling ones. Obtaining it from them is likely to depend on compulsion, and only too often their interrogation assumes repugnant forms. During the Philippine Insurrection some Americans had recourse to the "water cure" and other forms of torture, under which some of the victims died.[37] In the Philippines during World War II the Japanese used a screening process known among Filipinos as *zona:* Japanese troops would surround a place and assemble its inhabitants, who then were confronted by secret informants wearing hoods who silently pointed to those they were accusing of being Hukbalahaps or Huk supporters; the treatment accorded to those who were accused, meted out on the spot before the assembled community, was apt to be brutal in the extreme.[38] During the 1954–62 war in Algeria, the French also used hooded informants. In addition, they made extensive use of torture as an accompaniment of interrogation, usually in detention centers where others being held had to endure the screams of those undergoing it.[39]

It is well known that while interrogation under torture may yield some valid intelligence, it can also extort from victims, desperate to save themselves further agony, much information that is false—indeed, in at least one case of which I am aware, so much as to overwhelm those responsible for its collation.[40] In Algeria, the use of such measures, notably under General Jacques Massu, in his efforts to stamp out organized urban terrorism in Algiers, did much to create hatred for the French on the part of the Algerian people. It profoundly unsettled many French soldiers who heard about, witnessed, or were made to participate in acts of torture. It led Secretary-General Paul Teitgen of the Algiers prefecture, who recognized on detainees the marks of tortures he had himself undergone at the hands of the Gestapo, to submit his resignation in protest. Meanwhile, in France it was creating a revulsion against the war that helped undermine support for its continuance. As Teitgen is said to have remarked: "All right, Massu won the battle of Algiers; but that meant losing the war."[41]

I have already referred to the concept of insurgencies as having three possible phases: the first, one of preparation and organization; the second that of guerrilla warfare; and a third in which both sides engage in conventional operations. Except in those cases in which insurgency arises spontaneously, as it may, for example, in opposition to a foreign invader, the role of the leaders who prepare and organize it is clearly crucial: as Mao Zedong once observed, "If there is to be a revolution, there must be a revolutionary party."[42] There also can be no question but that the transformation of guerrilla forces into regular armies and employing those armies in battles of position and maneuver, in the third phase of an insurgency, calls for a centralized command. Thus, in the final stage of the Chinese civil war, the Communists formed a so-called front committee in preparation for the decisive campaign that began late in 1948 and was fought on the North China Plain. The committee was composed of the principal officers of two armies created from what had been guerrilla forces; they planned the campaign, and the political commissar of one of the two armies assumed responsibility for logistics.[43] It was only after that campaign had ended and resistance elsewhere in North China had been eliminated that the top leaders—who had divided into two groups and gone into hiding against the possibility of capture—emerged from their places of refuge and began the formation of what would become the government of the People's Republic of China.[44]

In the second, or guerrilla, stage of an insurgency the actively important roles are those played by great numbers of cadres of less than highest political rank working in a context of organizational decentralization. This decentralization makes it impossible for enemy intelligence to locate any key link in the insurgents' chain of command, because there is no such link to be found. Thus in the Spain of the Peninsular War, the political leadership of the insurgency was shared by a number of juntas that proved ineffective, were harried from place to place, and quarreled among themselves, while guerrilla bands recognized no authority but their own.[45] In the 1954–62 Algerian war for independence, the political leaders were outside the country, contended among themselves for top position, and found themselves bitterly opposed by the commanders of the guerrilla forces within Algeria, forces organized into autonomous commands without any central headquarters. More recently, in El Salvador, disparate guerrilla forces—variously Maoist, Trotskyite, and "proletarian" in their tendencies—which took to the field beginning in 1974, joined together only in 1980 to form the Farabundo Martí National Liberation Front, but failed to merge their forces under a common command.[46]

Finally, whether or not there is unity at the top, in the phase of guerrilla warfare there can only be decentralization of command and dispersion of both guerrilla forces and their sources of support, so that gathering and utilizing specific intelligence about them are tasks of almost infinite detail.

During the Vietnam War, the Combined Intelligence Center of MACV came to receive about three million documents a month, a large proportion captured in the course of military operations against the Viet Cong. About one-tenth were deemed worth translating, and at the beginning of 1967 upward of half a ton of reports based on them were being printed every day.[47] This huge harvest can have had but limited relevance to the military operations conducted by General Westmoreland. His preference was for large-scale operations directed against main force units of the Viet Cong and of the People's Army of Vietnam (PAVN), elements of which had been infiltrated from North Vietnam. These might require as much as four months of planning and preparation and employ forces comprising two divisions or more.[48] The Viet Cong and PAVN units against which they were directed usually stayed in rugged, forested terrain near the borders of Cambodia and Laos, where they operated in what might be described as guerrilla fashion writ large, and they proved difficult to engage.[49]

The quantities of intelligence available, however, made it possible to gain a relatively full picture of the organizational structure of the insurgency. This encouraged American civilian officials in Vietnam, notably personnel of the Central Intelligence

Agency, to develop what became known as the Phoenix program, directed against the political infrastructure of the insurgency.[50] That infrastructure, known as the National Liberation Front (NLF), was dominated by the communist People's Revolutionary Party (PRP). It shared its headquarters not only with the PRP, but also with the high command of the People's Liberation Army, better known as the Viet Cong. Because the PRP was an offshoot of North Vietnam's Communist Party, the Lao Dong, MACV and the American press referred to that headquarters as the Central Office for South Vietnam (COSVN). Below it were two elements, one organized vertically, the other horizontally. The vertical element ranged downward through four other levels to that of the villages, where its cadres were responsible for the horizontal element of the overall structure. It existed only at that level and was composed of mass organizations—the most important being those of farmers, of youths, and of women—the leaders of which formed village liberation committees. It was these organizations that provided support to the Viet Cong in the form of intelligence, guides, food, clothing, and recruits. This infrastructure was an adaptation of the Chinese communist model, in which some cadres organized several levels of a de facto government while others set up the mass organizations on which the People's Liberation Army depended for support. In addition, in all parts of South Vietnam, there was a Viet Cong security service that carried out assassinations and abductions, arrested and interrogated suspects, and carried out sentences.[51]

Among the Americans responsible for planning and initiating the Phoenix program, the infrastructure was believed to be the Viet Cong's jugular, and the leaders and important cadres of the infrastructure were seen as essential to its functioning.[52] The program was initiated about the beginning of 1968 and was conducted with the help of between six and seven hundred American advisers. The information it developed was turned over to military, police, and other officials of the Saigon government for action; their participation in the program was only part of their responsibilities, but there were also special armed formations known as Provincial Reconnaissance Units, totaling some 4,500 men, who served in the program full time.[53] As a management technique, the Vietnamese organizations engaged in the program were assigned monthly quotas of members of the NLF infrastructure who were to be put out of action. During its first year the judicial and correctional systems were incapable of dealing with the approximately 13,500 prisoners the Phoenix program produced, and many were released shortly after being apprehended.[54] In the several years of its existence, the program assertedly accounted for about 17,000 members of the Viet Cong infrastructure who had been amnestied, 20,000 who had been killed, and 28,000 who had been captured and, in the majority of cases, sentenced to imprisonment.[55]

Despite all the intelligence effort devoted to the program, only about 2 percent of those claimed as having been eliminated from the infrastructure had been specifically targeted: the names and whereabouts of the vast majority of its personnel simply were not known. Indeed, nine out of ten of those killed, many of them in the course of military operations, were killed anonymously, and only later identified—or misidentified—as members of the infrastructure.[56] While it was under way, the Phoenix program did not appear to affect Viet Cong operations or their level of support, and it came to be seen as ineffective. However, in more recent years Communists in South Vietnam have been quoted as saying that the Phoenix program cost them so many southern cadres that agents from North Vietnam had to be sent in to rebuild the infrastructure—agents who stayed on after the war to impose an unwelcome northern rule.[57] Though it may seem so, this assertion that the program did much damage to the infrastructure is not necessarily inconsistent with its apparent failure to affect the level of support of the Viet Cong, and hence their operations. If the people who constitute the mass base of an insurgency are committed to it and know what is expected of them, their support activities may continue more or less unaffected by damage to the infrastructure. Moreover, at the village level the infrastructure was highly decentralized and could operate autonomously, regardless of what happened to cadres of the vertically organized command structure.[58]

It was believed in American circles that the most important possible coup would be the capture of COSVN, the top communist headquarters in South Vietnam. Douglas Pike, an officer of the U.S. Information Service and a foremost authority on the Viet Cong, had reported as early as 1966 that COSVN personnel did not stay together in a single location—or, indeed, even in the same province.[59] Nevertheless, capture of that headquarters was an objective of one major operation by U.S. forces in 1967 and another in 1970. On the second occasion, President Nixon announced its imminent capture to the press, but when U.S. forces reached the supposed site of the headquarters, they found only a scattering of empty huts from which the occupants, in anticipation of the operation, had fled some weeks before.[60] Indeed, it clearly had been no highly organized command complex, nor is there reason to think that its personnel were irreplaceable.

The Political Factor in the Counterinsurgency Equation

Insurgencies, as we have seen, cannot prosper in the absence of a cause that enlists the support of a populace, and they accordingly are symptoms of ills of the body politic. They are not only conducted for political ends: they are also conducted by political as well as military means, and these circumstances cannot be without their relevance to the planning and conduct of counterinsurgencies. Because it is common, in conducting counterinsurgency operations, to employ a variety of means, some seriatim, others simultaneously, it may well be difficult, if not impossible, to judge how much each contributes to the outcome, whether it be success or failure. In the course of a number of insurgencies, however, the addition of political measures has marked a turning point, suggesting that they served as a necessary catalyst.

The ends sought in all wars of the third kind concern the governance of the lands in which they are waged. In the long run, a people can be governed only with their consent—preferably accorded willingly, at a minimum grudgingly given. As Edmund Burke warned the British Parliament in 1775, "The use of force alone is but temporary. It may subdue for a moment . . . but . . . a nation is not governed which is perpetually to be conquered."[61] Implicit in his warning was the recognition that resolution of a war of the third kind—as distinguished from mere suppression of armed resistance—requires that the cause or causes that gave rise to it be recognized and constructively dealt with.

The historian John F. Baddeley ascribed the rise of Imam Shamyl, who for thirty years led tribes of the eastern Caucasus in their resistance to imperial Russia, to the cruelties practiced against them by General Mihail Yermolov, and declared that the way was prepared for the final success of Russia by Shamyl's own dependence on terror for the maintenance of an exacting discipline.[62]

Yermolov had sought to make his name feared by such acts as driving ramrods through the ears of prisoners and auctioning off the women of villages as a form of collective punishment.[63] In the conquest of Kabarda, in the central Caucasus, he employed the strategy of devastation and depopulation.[64] In the eastern Caucasus Yermolov conquered much of Dagestan, a land of deep precipices and formidable peaks, but disunited because split into numerous khanates and independent communities,[65] and carried fire and sword into adjacent Tchetchnia, a region of great beech forests where there was no system of government whatsoever.[66] Those campaigns evoked the call for a jihad, issued in 1829 by Imam Khazi Mollah, Shamyl's predecessor, to which the peoples of the two regions responded in a common struggle against the forces led by Yermolov and his successors.[67]

It became the aim of Shamyl to extend this process of unified resistance to the Caucasus as a whole, first bringing under his banner the Cherkess, or Circassians, of the western Caucasus and then retaking the central region of Kabarda. However, the representative Shamyl maintained with the Circassians attempted to play off one tribe against another, enforced his authority with terrible severity, instigated massacres in the name of discipline, and eventually turned all Circassians against him.[68] Without their active collaboration on the west, Shamyl's invasion of Kabarda proved a failure. Moreover, Shamyl, too, used terror to maintain discipline: a tall, black-clad executioner wielding an axe and two sword bearers, each carrying a num-

ber of freshly sharpened blades, accompanied Shamyl every-
where, ready at the gesture of his hand to carry out such sentences as he might impose.[69]

With the appointment in 1856 of Prince Alexander Bariatinsky as Russian commander in chief, the situation in which the
peoples of Dagestan and Tchetchnia found themselves began to
change. Besides consistently employing the strategy of siege
for the first time, Bariatinsky conducted his campaigns along
quite different lines. His troops, upon taking a village, no
longer slaughtered the women, children, the old, and the in-
firm.[70] Civil administration in conquered places was placed in
the hands of locally elected leaders, and the people were helped
to rebuild their dwellings, restore their fields, and replenish
their herds. Once they realized that surrender would place
them beyond Shamyl's wrath, whole districts of war-weary
people surrendered, and in 1859, surrounded on a high ridge
with a mere four hundred men, Shamyl himself surrendered.[71]
(The Circassians, fighting their own war, held out against the
Russians some five years more, after which about three hundred thousand of them, rather than fall under non–Moslem
rule, fled to Turkey—an event paralleled in the flight of a substantial proportion of the Afghan population to Pakistan in the
1980s. As the Circassians departed, it is said, each man fired his
gun three times in a salute to his native mountains.)[72]

An example similar to that of the Caucasus is provided by
the suppression in 1795 of the rebellion in the Vendée against
the new republican government of France. The peasants of the
Vendée, devoutly Catholic, became enemies of the French
Revolution when it turned against the church, and in 1793 roy-
alist leaders were able to raise an army of some fifty thousand
there and to begin clearing the region of republican authorities.
However, by the end of that year, the Vendéan army, which
attempted to fight positional battles, had suffered total defeat.
The rebellion appeared to be finished, but while it was still
going on the Committee of Public Safety ordered the removal
of women and children from the Vendée to the interior, the
burning of its villages, the destruction of its crops, the seizure
of its cattle, and the cutting down of its forests. In January
1784, those orders not having been rescinded, General Louis

Marie Turreau ordered his troops to complete the devastation of the Vendée and to put to the bayonet all people encountered who were suspected of taking part in the rebellion, not excluding such woman and children as remained.[73]

In assigning that mission to his troops, Turreau called it a "ten-day promenade," expecting that it would deal the final blow to a dying war. Instead, he rekindled the rebellion throughout the countryside, where it assumed the character of a guerrilla war.[74] In May Turreau was withdrawn, but succeeded by other commanders whose methods were similar and who made no progress in suppressing the rebellion. A change came, however, after the accession to power in Paris in the summer of 1794 of a moderate faction that recognized that there would have to be a reconciliation with the people of the Vendée if they were to be ruled, and its economy would have to be rebuilt if it were to support its people and yield needed revenues. In December it announced an amnesty, in February 1795 it granted the people of the Vendée freedom of worship and some indemnification for the losses they had suffered, and the following August it assigned General Louis Lazare Hoche to the Vendée.[75]

Upon assuming command, Hoche stopped the burning of villages and the destruction of crops. The people were required to turn in their arms, and if they did not comply, their cattle were seized and returned only in exchange for their weapons. The soldiers were forbidden to pillage, and commanders who permitted them to do so were punished by demotion. In his troops Hoche instilled a spirit of the offensive: those approaching the enemy close enough were required to charge with the bayonet; in open country the guerrillas were pursued relentlessly by detachments of light infantry and cavalry; and after ten days in the field, those units were withdrawn and replaced by fresh troops. At the same time Hoche, although himself anticlerical, restored the priests to the churches, and when some of them expressed distrust of his sincerity, he invited them to perform mass in his own quarters. The farmers, helped to reestablish themselves, stopped supporting the guerrillas, the ranks of the rebels dwindled, and by the end of 1795 the Vendée was at peace.[76]

"A doctrine of counterguerrilla warfare," Samuel P. Huntington has written, "is a necessary but not sufficient doctrine in the struggle against revolutionary forces. . . . To win a revolutionary war, it is necessary to carry on a prolonged campaign for the support of a key social group."[77] In the case of the Hukbalahap rebellion in the Philippines, the heartland of which was Luzon's central plain, the key social group was the peasantry of the region, and the decisive changes that won its support and reversed a deteriorating situation were those introduced by Ramon Magsaysay. During the period preceding his assumption of the post of defense secretary, in which the government depended almost exclusively on armed force in its efforts to suppress the Hukbalahap, a military formation known as the Nenita, or Skull Unit, commanded by Colonel Napoleon Valeriano, became greatly feared and won a reputation for outstanding dash and effectiveness. In the early 1960s, as though reflecting on the futility that may attend the use of good military tactics in the service of a bad overall strategy, Valeriano wrote that "the effect of the Nenita operation, and of the reputation it gained throughout the country, was on the whole to increase support for the Huk."[78]

Magsaysay, in keeping with a promise he made to the Huks of all-out friendship or all-out force, continued to press the armed struggle vigorously. His operations showed an appreciation of the fact that search and destroy operations by small, lightly armed and highly mobile detachments have a greater chance of achieving surprise than sweeps by large, heavily armed bodies of troops and will do less harm to the local people and less damage to their property. At the same time, those operations reflected awareness that a single small detachment of soldiers cannot be expected to operate on its own in areas where guerrillas are in close rapport with the populace and capable of rapidly gathering for combat, while operations conducted by numerous small detachments pose problems of coordination. However, those difficulties proved not to be insurmountable: for example, Magsaysay used a technique of so saturating an area with patrols that the Huks' intelligence network became overloaded. He also combined large- and small-scale operations, assigning small units the task of intercepting guerrillas the operations of large units had dislodged.[79]

In keeping with his offer of all-out friendship, as the alternative to all-out force, Magsaysay gave Huks willing to surrender amnesty, and for those unwilling to return to their former places of residence, where they perhaps had made enemies, help in resettling on Mindanao. According to both rebels and non-rebels, Magsaysay cleaned up the army and the constabulary; at his insistence a beginning was made in implementing agrarian reforms; and, thanks in large part to his determination, the army saw to it that the elections of 1951 were peaceful and honestly conducted—opening the way to peaceful change as an alternative to revolution. In consequence, the organized support structure the Huks had created withered and the number of Huks dwindled.[80]

What Magsaysay did in the twentieth-century Philippines and Hoche in the Vendée of the late eighteenth century was to deal successfully with fellow nationals. What Bariatinsky accomplished in the Caucasus was to suppress the resistance of a grouping of small khanates, feuding tribes, and independent communities, serving under a common leader. Suppressing a national war of resistance waged by a united people against a foreign invader is a problem of quite different magnitude, as reflected by the comment of one writer that it is easier for guerrilla movements to succeed against foreigners, however strong, than against indigenous governments, however weak.[81]

The famous strategist Antoine Henri de Jomini, writing before the present age of nationalism, speculated on the question of whether it was possible to win a war like that of Napoleon against the guerrillas in Spain. If it were possible, he said, it would have to be by methods like those used by Marshal Louis Gabriel Suchet, who gained great repute as a fair administrator while serving as governor of Catalonia during the Peninsular War, and whom Jomini likened to Hoche in the Vendée. It would be necessary, Jomini wrote, "to make a display of a mass of troops proportioned to the obstacles and resistance likely to be encountered, calm the popular passions in every possible way, exhaust them by time and patience, display courtesy, gentleness and severity united, and, particularly, deal justly."[82]

In summary, as I remarked near the beginning of this chapter, counterinsurgency operations can have as their targets the armed insurgents themselves, the noncombatants and material means by which the insurgents are supported, and the organizational infrastructure on which they depend for purposes of command and of mustering popular support. I also observed that approaches to insurgency may treat the populace from which guerrillas derive their support as enemies; may ignore its relevance to the outcome of the struggle, or treat it as of only secondary importance; or may recognize that gaining and holding the support of the people is the key to deciding the struggle.

Attempting to find, fix, and fight guerrilla insurgents by attacking particular places, in the expectation of their being defended, and carrying out search-and-destroy missions in populated areas—especially on a repetitive basis and with the use of such nonselective weapons as tanks, artillery, and aerial bombing—is to miscalculate the relevance of noncombatants and their attitudes to the outcome of the struggle. Moreover, to conduct such operations is to wage a war of attrition favorable to guerrillas, who can usually accept or avoid combat as they choose and thus keep their casualties below the level of their replacement capabilities. The policy of forcing rural people from their homes and of devastating the countryside from which they have been removed, to the extent that it can be carried out in practice, obviously deprives guerrillas of a proportionate amount of support. It does so at the cost of commensurate damage to the economy and social fabric of the area to which it is applied and of the enmity of its people.

Clear-and-hold operations can have the advantages of avoiding the cumulative damage imposed by the repetition of search-and-destroy missions, of preventing guerrillas from having further access to the people of such areas as have been cleared, and of providing the opportunity to apply such political measures in those areas as may serve to win the positive loyalty of the people. The clear-and-hold operations discussed above, whether directed against an enclave or from one, were geographically well defined, but their objective of separating populace and insurgents can be pursued in other contexts and by other means.

One such means is identifying, locating, and apprehending the people essential to the directing and support of the insurgency—the key personnel of its organizational infrastructure.

It is during the preparatory phase of an insurgency that its leaders are most vulnerable to arrest. In its second phase, with the need for decentralization and dispersal in guerrilla warfare, the organizational activities that matter most are those of cadres at the grass-roots level, and it has yet to be demonstrated that they can be identified and apprehended in decisive numbers under conditions of internal war. In its guerrilla phase, the top leaders of an insurgency are of limited relevance; for security reasons they are unlikely all to remain together; and even if captured or killed—as were eight of the nine top leaders of the 1954–62 insurgency in Algeria—their places will be taken by others.[83] If a time comes for judging the feasibility of passing from guerrilla to conventional war, the decision will be theirs, but if they prove right, the time for trying to apprehend them will be past.

As some of the above examples have demonstrated, an insurgency and its infrastructure may prove vulnerable to an approach in which military and political measures are combined. In some instances credit was due largely or wholly to a capable military commander who happened to be endowed with much political feel: in this context, the cases of Bariatinsky in the Caucasus and Hoche in the Vendée come to mind. In others it has been possible because the counterinsurgency was conducted under a political leadership that benefited from the close cooperation of the military. That was true of the anti-Huk campaign in the Philippines under Magsaysay and of the British suppression under the control of a government committee of the post–World War II communist insurgency in Malaya.

Magsaysay brought to the task an unusual combination of relevant experience and personal determination, while the British in Malaya benefited from a long tradition of military responsiveness to political authority. General Douglas Kinnard, who was one of the American commanders in Vietnam, has remarked that although it is the civilians in the United States who ultimately are in charge, there has been a long-standing tradition of an adversary relationship between American civilian and military leaders, and that it continued during the war in Indochina.[84] U. Alexis Johnson, deputy chief of mission in Saigon during the ambassadorship of General Taylor, put the same problem somewhat differently. The challenge of counter-insurgency, he wrote in his memoirs, is its requirement that the political and military sectors be harmonized at both tactical and strategic levels. At the national level, he continued, we harmonize political goals and military capabilities badly enough, and at the tactical level not at all.[85]

6 The Perils for the Powers of Small Wars

Wars of the third kind, besides devastating the lands in which they are fought, can pose serious dangers to powers that become involved in them. These risks are of two kinds: they can lead to military disaster, and they can undermine the polity of the state. These dangers arise from initial underestimation of the problems that wars against the weak can pose for the strong, and subsequent inability to bring them to a successful conclusion.

Frustration over inability to bring a war of the third kind to a successful conclusion and unwillingness to cut their losses tend to cause a country's leaders to look beyond the theater in which it is being fought for the root of their difficulties. In doing so they are likely both to extend the geographic scope of the conflict and to enlarge the dimensions of their problem. Leadership implies an ability to choose right paths, whereas turning back would imply admission of error. Because such admissions are seldom willingly made, it is in the democracies, with their freedom of the press, their competition between political parties, and their provisions for the peaceful transfer of power, that there is the best chance of abandoning a wrong course before it ends in disaster.

George C. Marshall once declared that a democracy cannot fight a seven-year war, a statement that suggests that a democracy that attempts to do so runs the risk of ceasing to be one. What he no doubt had in mind was the prospect that the pressures for conformity and the curtailment of press freedom attending a state of war, if too prolonged, might lead to a permanent situation in which the people were no longer the masters of their government. Marshall's statement was made in the context of World War II, when publication of information about troop movements might lead to ship sinkings and the disclosure of strategic plans might result in the loss of battles. In wars of the third kind, however, such considerations have little relevance, and the temptation to impose press censorship is likely to arise from the wish to keep embarrassing information from the public and thus to minimize dissent. In the case of the United States, press censorship motivated by such considerations must be viewed against the background of the provision of the Constitution prohibiting curtailment of the freedom of the press.

The theses that frustration over inability to bring a war of the third kind to a successful conclusion, combined with unwillingness to abandon it, can lead a powerful country to military disaster, that censorship during a war of the third kind may arise from political calculation rather than military necessity, and that the political system of a powerful country can be endangered by entanglement in such a war, may be explored in a number of contexts: the Sino-Japanese war, the Algerian war for independence, the Philippine Insurrection, and the Vietnam conflict.

Pre–World War II Japan, an imperialist power ruling Korea and holding leased territory in Manchuria, had become a state dominated by the army. During the early 1930s the Japanese army had driven Chinese armed forces from the rest of Manchuria, where it had set up the puppet state of Manchukuo. The Japanese military next began efforts to transform five provinces of North China into a special region independent of the nationalist government at Nanking. It wanted to avoid war, but in 1937 the Japanese program of piecemeal conquest met resistance from provincial Chinese troops.

The fighting began near Peking on 7 July, and in August the

Japanese, believing that resistance in North China had outside inspiration and could be ended by defeating Chiang Kai-shek's armies and seizing his capital, landed troops at Shanghai and attempted to drive inland. Chiang's forces put up a stout positional defense until November, when the Japanese turned their flank by making an amphibious landing farther south in Hangchow Bay. In December, with the broken nationalist armies in retreat and the Japanese about to take Nanking, Chiang Kai-shek moved his government to Chungking, beyond the formidable rapids of the Yangtze in the mountain-encircled western province of Szechwan.

Chiang Kai-shek having eluded them, the Japanese next began efforts to isolate his government in Szechwan from outside support. By the end of 1938, through a campaign climaxed by the capture of the port of Canton in South China and of central China's strategic tricity complex of Wuhan, the Japanese had gained control of most of China's principal cities and main transport lines. As a conventional conflict, the war was over, and what followed was a long period of semi-passive resistance by the remaining regular forces of Chiang Kai-shek and active harassment at the hands of growing numbers of communist guerrillas.

The Japanese now found themselves in a situation much like that envisaged in 1793 by Lord Macartney, who visited China as envoy of George III. In discussing the probable consequences of an attempt to conquer the Chinese, he wrote: "The circumstance of greatest embarrassment to an invader would be their immense numbers, not on account of the mischief they could do to him, but that he would find no end of doing mischief to them . . . and, unless the people themselves voluntarily submitted, the victor might indeed reap the vanity of destruction, but not the glory or use of dominion."[1] Indeed, the Japanese had bitten off more than they could chew and badly wanted a peace settlement. But while it takes only one to make war, two are needed to make peace, and Chiang Kai-shek rejected all their overtures.

In time, and not completely without reason, the Japanese came to see the United States as chiefly responsible for Chiang's unwillingness to make peace. The Japanese had not declared war and called the conflict "the China Incident." President Franklin D. Roosevelt clearly was referring to it in his "Quarantine" speech of 5 October 1937, when he warned that war is "a contagion, whether it be declared or undeclared," which "can engulf states and peoples remote from the original scene of hostilities." In December 1938 the United States began extending financial assistance to the Chinese government, and in July 1939, in order to put itself in a position to take a variety of economic measures against Japan, it gave notice of intent not to renew the Japan–U.S. treaty of commerce and navigation upon its expiration the following year. Early in 1941 the United States approved a plan under which army and navy airmen were released from service and supplied with fighter planes in order that they might help fight the Japanese in China as members of what was called the American Volunteer Group. It was also decided that China should receive military aid under the recently passed Lend–Lease Act.[2]

During this period of drift toward war between Japan and the United States, some concerned Americans and Japanese succeeded in promoting the initiation of a series of informal talks between Secretary of State Cordell Hull and Japanese Ambassador Kichisaburo Nomura, which had as their aim the restoration of good relations between the two countries. On 18 April 1941, shortly after the first of those talks had been held, the Japanese government received from Nomura a telegram containing a list of matters at issue and a draft understanding for adoption by the two governments by which they might be settled. The draft understanding provided, among other things, that the American president would advise Chiang Kai-shek to open peace negotiations with Japan on a basis that would have required his government to recognize Manchukuo and to accept amalgamation with a puppet regime the Japanese had recently set up in Nanking. Although no one in Tokyo knew it at the time, the draft understanding had been written by a Japanese colonel on temporary duty in the Japanese embassy in Washington, which had not yet discussed it with officials of the U.S. government. Indeed, it was to be more than a month before its true status became known to Japanese officials in Tokyo.[3]

On the day the telegram was received, Premier Fumimaro

Konoye called a meeting attended by the principal members of his cabinet, excepting only Foreign Minister Yosuke Matsuoka, then en route home from a mission in Europe, as well as by the chiefs of staff of the army and the navy. According to Konoye, it was the prevailing reaction of those present that an agreement along the lines proposed in the message offered the means whereby the China affair could be satisfactorily disposed of. Nothing could be achieved through strictly bilateral negotiations with Chungking, but because the Chinese government was "entirely dependent on the United States," a settlement might be achieved with the United States serving as intermediary. In addition, it was important to respond favorably to the United States because Japan needed to avoid war with the United States and to recover from the resource drain incurred since the outbreak of "the China Incident."[4]

It was not until the latter part of May that it was understood in Japanese government circles that the proposal received the previous month had originated in the Japanese embassy in Washington, and another month passed before that government received the first American statement concerning the basis on which an understanding might be reached.[5] It included respect for the territorial integrity and sovereignty of each and every nation, support for the principle of non-interference in the internal affairs of other countries, and non-disturbance of the status quo in the Pacific except as it might be altered by peaceful means.[6] The application of those principles, it was made clear, would require Japan to withdraw its forces from China.[7]

In mid July the Japanese government sent Washington its counterproposals, which were based on the views of the army and the navy, but at the same time it moved to alter the status quo in French Indochina. The emperor had expressed distaste for the idea of "Japan's playing the thief at a fire," but had agreed to the move on the grounds that Japan had to cope with the tremendous changes then taking place in the world.[8] In 1940, in a short but sharp engagement against French forces, the Japanese had taken over the northern part of French Indochina. This had enabled them to prevent further use, as a supply route for the forces of Chiang Kai-shek, of the port of Haiphong and the narrow-gauge railway connecting it with

Kunming in China's southwestern province of Yunnan.[9] Now, taking advantage of the inability of the Vichy regime to protect French interests abroad, the Japanese negotiated with it for an unopposed entry of Japanese forces into southern Indochina. The U.S. government having learned of the negotiations, Ambassador Nomura was called to the State Department and told that Japanese occupation of southern Indochina would destroy the utility of the ongoing talks between Japan and the United States. The Japanese nevertheless went ahead, occupying the naval base at Cam Ranh Bay and eight airfields in striking distance of the Philippines, Malaya, and the Dutch East Indies.[10]

Within about forty-eight hours of the first Japanese landings, the United States, Great Britain, and the Netherlands took action to freeze Japanese assets. Then on 1 August, with the Japanese operation continuing, the United States and the Netherlands—the latter with respect to the Dutch East Indies—embargoed further shipments of oil to Japan.[11] This came as an unexpected blow, and also as a most serious one: Japan had no petroleum sources of its own, it had only limited capacity for the production of synthetic fuels, and the armed forces had on hand stocks that in case of war would last them less than eighteen months.[12]

The United States and its allies thus had a stranglehold on Japan. Its military leaders were willing that Konoye should attempt through diplomatic negotiations to get it loosened, but meanwhile they would prepare plans for moving farther south in order to gain control of the oilfields of the Dutch East Indies, and the rubber plantations, tin mines, and other sources of raw materials of Malaya and Burma. This would mean going to war with the United States and Great Britain, and Konoye would be given a short deadline. For reasons of seasonal weather to the south, military operations, if not begun by early in December, would have to be postponed until the following spring—by which time the oil situation would have become critical.[13]

Konoye and some of the others opposed these plans, holding that a war against the United States and Great Britain would be likely to bring disaster to Japan and might bring to an end the 2,600-year reign of its imperial family. Accordingly, they urged that negotiations be carried on without a deadline, that Japan expand its capacity for producing synthetic fuels as rapidly as possible, and that it meanwhile tighten its belt. They also suggested that Japan agree, at least in principle, to withdraw its troops from China, in the hope that this would induce the United States and its allies to withdraw the economic sanctions they had imposed.[14]

Nevertheless, on 4 September Konoye's cabinet gave its approval to a document prepared by the supreme command in which it was specified that if in early October there still was no prospect of Japan's attaining its demands through diplomatic negotiations, it would immediately open hostilities with the United States, Great Britain, and the Netherlands. This policy was to be presented at an imperial conference on 6 September, and in preparation for that meeting Konoye sought an audience with the emperor on 5 September. The emperor, Konoye found, was greatly concerned, and demanded to know why the document in question began with a section on war preparations, suggesting that they were being given precedence over diplomacy. The emperor also asked other questions, some of them related to military operations, and because Konoye could not answer them, he suggested that the two chiefs of staff be summoned. Accordingly, General Gen Sugiyama and Admiral Osami Nagano were called in, and when they arrived the emperor again asked whether the order in which matters were being dealt with did not suggest that war was being given precedence over diplomacy. Assured by the service chiefs that the order in which the items appeared was without significance, the emperor turned to Sugiyama and asked: "In case of an American-Japanese conflict, how many months does the army consider with confidence that it will take to dispose of the matter?" Answering the question only in part, Sugiyama replied: "So far as the southern area is concerned, we intend to settle things within the first three months." The emperor then declared: "At the time of the outbreak of the China affair, you were the war minister, and you said, 'The affair will be settled in a month or so.' And yet the affair has lasted four years and yet has not been settled."[15]

Sugiyama, greatly embarrassed, explained that China had a large hinterland area and offered other excuses, whereupon the emperor asked: "If you say China has a wide hinterland, the Pacific ocean is larger, isn't it? With what confidence do you say that it will take three months?" Sugiyama having lowered his head and failed to reply, Admiral Nagano spoke up, likening Japanese-American relations to a patient considering whether to have an operation. The patient is gradually weakening, but if he undergoes an operation, though it involves danger, there may be hope for his recovery. The high command hoped that a solution might be attained by diplomatic means, but in case of failure an operation would have to be performed. When Nagano had finished, the emperor asked whether the service chiefs meant to emphasize diplomacy as the way to solve the issues at stake, and they asserted that they did.[16]

The imperial conference held on 6 September to pass on the proposal discussed at the audience of the previous day was supposed to be a highly ritualistic affair. At such conferences, deemed part of the process by which policies were given imperial sanction, the emperor neither presided nor spoke, and they never failed to endorse the proposals laid before them.[17] Shortly before the 6 September conference, however, the emperor made it known to Koichi Kido, the keeper of the privy seal, that he would wish to raise questions designed to commit the participants to stressing diplomatic negotiations rather than preparations for war. However, Kido revealed that Dr. Yoshimichi Hara, the president of the privy council, had already been primed to ask such questions, and the initiative accordingly was left to him. During the conference, and after the formal presentations had been completed, Dr. Hara raised anew the question of the order in which matters had been presented in the document before the conference. The two service chiefs, who had just completed their presentations, retained their places, but Admiral Koshino Oikawa, the navy minister, immediately arose and affirmed that the order in which items had been presented was without significance, that every effort was to be made to settle matters through diplomacy, and that Japan would go to war only if those efforts failed. At this point the emperor, breaking the silence that tradition demanded, expressed regret that it had not been the representatives of the supreme command who had responded to Dr. Hara, and drew from his pocket a piece of paper from which he read aloud a poem composed by his grandfather, Emperor Meiji. In the poem Meiji recalled the Confucian saying that all within the four seas are brothers and asked why, then, the winds and waves of strife were raging so turbulently throughout the world. Having read the poem, the emperor observed that it was a favorite of his and that his efforts were directed toward introducing in his own time the spirit of Meiji's love of peace.[18]

The emperor's intercession was said to have had an overwhelming effect on those present, but in the days that followed Konoye found himself unable to form his cabinet into a united front for the purpose of opposing the positions of the supreme command, which remained essentially unchanged. He won the lukewarm support of Admiral Oikawa but failed utterly to reach an accord with General Hideki Tojo, the minister of war. Japan, Tojo declared, could not meet the U.S. demand for the withdrawal of Japanese troops from China. They were needed there, he said, for the good of both countries, because the Chinese interior was plagued by communist guerrillas and other lawless elements. Moreover, if Japanese troops were withdrawn from China the resulting loss of prestige would spread from China to Manchuria and Korea. In view of Tojo's attitude, Konoye decided, successful negotiations with the United States were impossible, and the cabinet would have to resign.[19]

Because of peculiarities in the Japanese governmental system, it would not do to simply ask Tojo to resign. In Japan the supreme command was not responsible to the government as represented by the premier and his cabinet. Each cabinet had to have a war minister and a navy minister drawn from among generals and admirals who were in active service, which meant that they were responsive to the supreme command. Indeed, the supreme command could bring down a cabinet by withdrawing a service minister or prevent the formation of a new cabinet by not making one available.[20] Had Konoye requested the resignation of Tojo, another general might have been provided as his successor. However, because Tojo's views and those of the army command were in accord, Konoye would hardly have found the new man more amenable.

The Konoye cabinet resigned on 16 October and Japan's senior statesmen, in their search for a successor, finally settled on Tojo—partly because of objections to everyone else they considered and partly because it was thought he was thoroughly loyal to the emperor and could control the army. The emperor had remained firm and was now making the unprecedented demand that in deciding the policies that should thenceforth guide the state, the next cabinet make a thoroughgoing study of the situation at home and abroad—without being bound by the decision taken at the imperial conference of 6 September.[21]

Tojo accepted the emperor's injunction that the slate be wiped clean and relevant policy formulated afresh. However, Tojo's perceptions had not changed, nor had those of the supreme command. They were men impatient of obstacles, whose training emphasized decisive action, and in their circles those assailed by doubts were unlikely to give them expression. Though in theory the service chiefs were subordinate to the emperor, much as the prime minister was, the emperor was supposed to reign but not rule, and he lacked the staff arrangements that supervision of the military would have required. Thus it was that Japan's final position, which Ambassador Nomura was on 20 November instructed to present to Secretary Hull, was one Nomura thought would only make matters worse. In Southeast Asia and the South Pacific, Japan would undertake to advance no farther by force. For its part, the United States was to guarantee that Japan's needs for oil would be met through a restoration of the conditions that had existed before the freezing of Japanese assets, and the United States was to agree not to obstruct the restoration of peace between China and Japan by continuing its support of Chiang Kai-shek. Within the Japanese government it was agreed that if no settlement had been reached by 1 December, the decision for war would be made, regardless of the state of negotiations at that time.[22]

On 29 November, at a meeting with an advisory council composed of ex-premiers, Tojo said that by knocking out the American Pacific Fleet and seizing the resources of Southeast Asia, Japan would gain control of a self-sufficient area that could be defended in depth. The Americans would be forced to see the hopelessness of their struggle, and the conflict might be quickly ended.[23] This was the kind of success that Japan had achieved in the Russo-Japanese War, begun without a declaration of war with a surprise attack in February 1904 on Port Arthur, where the Russian fleet was concentrated, and ended the following year by the Treaty of Portsmouth. In this case the emperor asked that the first act of war not take place until the Japanese had broken off negotiations in Washington, intending that this should serve as a declaration of war. However, the navy's plans for the attack on Pearl Harbor and a subsequent safe withdrawal of the Japanese fleet depended on achieving surprise. In the event, the emperor's request was not honored, and the Japanese commander of the first wave of attacking planes, seeing through a rift in the clouds that the American fleet below was lying peacefully at anchor, is said to have asked himself whether the Americans had never heard of Port Arthur.[24]

With the attack on Pearl Harbor the Japanese had extended their military operations five thousand miles from North China and had converted the "China Affair" into what they called the "War for Greater East Asia," a war that brought to Japan wholesale destruction, military defeat, and the humbling experience of military occupation. (Actually, much of the all-encompassing destruction wreaked on Japan, according to what I was taught at the National War College, was militarily unnecessary. In this view, destruction of any vital link in the chain of Japan's capacity to wage war would have sufficed, and the key link—a view that accorded with that of Japan's former supreme command—was the petroleum supply.)

One member of Tojo's cabinet was doubtless speaking for many others when he declared, in the wake of Japan's defeat, that the "War for Greater East Asia" had been the greatest disaster in the long history of Japan. Nevertheless, it brought in its train changes that all but ultranationalist Japanese can only regard as beneficial. Beginning in the early 1930s, fanatical chauvinists, most of them army officers of the middle and lower grades, had with their jingoistic propaganda and frequent resort to political assassination created an atmosphere in which the decision to expand the China war seemed inevitable. The defeat and occupation of Japan discredited them and created a change of political atmosphere, and in this altered situation it became possible to eliminate the ambiguous situation in which the military were nominally subordinate to the emperor but in practice a law unto themselves. This was accomplished through the adoption of constitutional amendments defining the status of the emperor as that of symbol of the state and of the unity of the Japanese people and establishing the supremacy of an elective parliament.[25]

In the wake of World War II, France became successively involved in two wars of the third kind. One ended in defeat, setting the stage for a second and more dangerous war that followed hard upon it. The first was the struggle against the Viet Minh in French Indochina, which began in 1946. It reached its climax in May 1954, when the Viet Minh, having gained the necessary conventional warfare capability, defeated the French in a set-piece battle at Dien Bien Phu, and was ended two months later with an armistice agreement signed at Geneva providing for the withdrawal of French forces. The second, the 1954–62 Algerian war for independence, broke out less than four months later. The French military brought to it a sense of frustration that was a legacy of Vietnam and a determination to succeed in Algeria by applying there what they believed to be Vietnam's lessons. In Algeria France was to commit over half a million troops, about twice as many as in that earlier struggle, and to it they were to devote far greater material resources.

In 1848, under the Second Republic, Algeria had been declared an integral part of France, and its territories had been organized into three provinces. Nevertheless, more than a century later Algerian Muslims, though French subjects at birth, generally could not become French citizens.[26] In 1954 Algeria contained, besides some nine million Muslims, over nine hundred thousand Europeans to whom Algeria was home in the sense of the phrase "Ici, c'est la France." By then the legal fiction that Algeria was not a colony was more than a century old and was being held more tenaciously than ever because under armed challenge. In this connection I recall that while serving in Germany I attended a luncheon addressed by an eminent French politician who informed us that Algeria's status as an

integral part of France made granting Algerian demands for independence impossible—a statement that was received with a
quietness I took to denote respectful disbelief.

The Algerian rebellion began on 1 November 1954, and it
had not been under way for two years before officials in Paris,
yielding to the urge to look further afield for the solution to
troubles close at hand, focused their attention on Egypt. And
not without provocation: the first proclamation of the revolutionary FLN—the Front de Libération Nationale—had been
broadcast by Cairo radio.[27] Gamal Abdel Nasser, Egypt's premier and a self-proclaimed pan-Arabist, ostentatiously offered
money and arms for the rebellion, though what he actually
supplied was negligible—a fact FLN leaders in Cairo kept secret in the interests of the morale of their fighters in Algeria.[28]
The French, too, were deceived: when Foreign Minister Christian Pineau visited Cairo, Nasser self-importantly declared that
when the French were ready to negotiate in Algeria, they should
let him know and matters would soon be settled.[29]

Based on such grounds, and on wishful thinking, Guy
Mollet, the French prime minister, and Maurice Bourges-
Maunoury, the defense minister, reached the conclusion that if
Nasser went, the collapse of the Algerian revolt would follow,
and in the autumn of 1956 events gave them the opportunity to
test its validity. Intending to counter the influence of Soviet-
bloc aid to Cairo, the United States and Great Britain had
offered financial aid to Egypt for the construction of the Aswan
High Dam. However, Nasser queered the deal by recognizing
the government of the People's Republic of China, Secretary of
State John Foster Dulles responded with a public rebuke, and
the United States and Britain withdrew their offers of aid. In
this situation, Great Britain was more vulnerable to a retaliatory blow from Nasser than was the United States. The stock-
holders of the privately owned and managed Suez Canal Company were predominantly British; Great Britain was dependent
on Middle Eastern oil, which reached it via Suez; that country
had for decades been guarantor of safe passage through the canal by the ships of all countries, and the last contingent of British troops had been withdrawn from the canal zone as recently

as June 1956. In July, following the withdrawal of the American and British aid offers, Nasser nationalized the canal.[30]

At the end of October Israel, which had been having its own troubles with Nasser, invaded Egyptian territory, and in November British troops—joined by French paratroopers drawn from the forces in Algeria—began an operation that had as its military objective the retaking of the Suez canal. However, the invasion immediately loosed a storm of opposition: from Moscow came dire threats, from Washington came expressions of disapproval, and from New York the censure of the United Nations. Forty hours after the beginning of their attack, the British and the French halted the advance of their troops, which were subsequently withdrawn.[31] The short war left the canal blocked by sunken ships, failed to discredit Nasser, led to the resignation of British Prime Minister Anthony Eden, and destroyed Mollet's hopes of victory in Algeria.

The FLN established its government in exile in adjacent Tunisia, which also provided a sanctuary where FLN troops could train and rest, as well as the most convenient route for arms supplies. In dealing with this situation, and a similar, though less urgent, problem along Algeria's border with Morocco, the French built the Morice Line along the Tunisian frontier, running 200 miles from the Mediterranean to the wastes of the Sahara. Consisting of a high electrified fence designed to kill on contact, with minefields on either side, the line had sensors that told when and where it had been broken and was constantly patrolled.[32] Designed to prevent rebel units and supplies from crossing into Algeria, it also kept the French from striking at rebel units and supply bases in Tunisia, as well as preventing them from pursuing rebels who inflicted casualties on French border patrols into that country. In consequence, French officers raised demands to extend the war into Tunisia, which came to a head early in 1958 after a French patrol had been ambushed by rebels believed to have crossed the line near the Tunisian village of Sakiet.[33] On two occasions French planes that flew over the village to investigate were hit by machine-gun fire, and on 8 February a squadron of bombers staged a retaliatory raid on the village. The timing was unfortunate, for it was market day in Sakiet. Moreover, besides hitting the FLN base, the bombs and rockets blasted a school where classes were in session and a hospital, as foreign journalists quickly ferried to the scene were able to testify. Tunisia accused France of aggression before the Security Council of the United Nations, and in the uproar they had inadvertently created, the demand of the French military for extending the war was drowned out.[34]

The French army, it will be appreciated, bore the unhappy memory of defeat in World War II, and that defeat had just been followed by the loss of Indochina. Many of the officers and men of the French army in Algeria had served in Indochina, and were determined not to lose another campaign.[35] The war in Indochina had been a highly political conflict, and many of the French officers who had taken part had been politicized by it. In addition, some among them, like some Germans after their country's World War I defeat, rationalized military failure with ill-defined notions that there had been treachery. The 1956 Suez misadventure had contributed to a feeling that the politicians were to blame for the troubles of the military, and there was among the military a fear that there would come to power in Paris a government that would decide to abandon Algeria, much as that of Pierre Mendès-France had given up Indochina. Meanwhile, Algeria's Europeans saw the French army standing between them and the loss of their all, and because they were in close rapport, the European civilians and French military reinforced each other's fears and suspicions. In consequence, Algiers, the country's political capital and military headquarters, was pervaded by an atmosphere of tension punctuated by plotted violence.[36]

On 13 May 1958 a mob of Europeans in Algiers staged a riot that was to lead to the fall of the Fourth Republic, under which France had been governed since shortly after the end of World War II, and the establishing of the Fifth Republic under a constitution providing for a strengthened executive. The mob sacked the headquarters of the civilian governor general, calling for the army to take power, a call that resulted in the creation on the spot of a Committee of Public Safety composed of military officers and leaders of the mob. That night Gaullists in the entourage of General Raoul Salan, the commander in chief in

Algeria, prevailed upon him to follow up his reporting of the day's events with a telegram to President René Coty urging the formation in France of a government of public safety headed by General de Gaulle. Some weeks previously, in the wake of the Sakiet affair, the government of Félix Gaillard had fallen, and on 14 May his successor, Pierre Pflimlin, invested by the Assembly by a better than two-to-one vote, assumed office. However, in Algiers the French military stood by the demand for de Gaulle's return to office, that demand was quickly taken up in Paris by his military and civilian followers, and on 19 May de Gaulle held a press conference at which he expressed readiness to assume power provided the political system of the Fourth Republic was swept away.[37]

Upon receiving news of de Gaulle's press conference, Salan sent another telegram to President Coty saying that unless de Gaulle assumed power as soon as possible, there might be a military incursion into metropolitan France. As a matter of fact, Salan already had planning for such an incursion under way; by 14 May paratroopers from Algeria had seized Corsica; on 28 May Pflimlin resigned; and the following day President Coty, having received a 29 May deadline from Salan, announced that de Gaulle had been asked to form a government. On 1 June de Gaulle appeared before the National Assembly, asking to be given full powers to govern for six months by decree, and a mandate to submit a new constitution for the approval of the country. The Assembly, although it undoubtedly anticipated that the new constitution would be one that reduced its powers, felt compelled to meet his terms.[38]

Upon assuming office, de Gaulle brought in a loyal supporter as chief of the general staff and gave him the task of scattering the group of officers in Algeria who had been responsible for the downfall of Pflimlin and his own return to power.[39] Salan was transferred to the sinecure post of military governor of Paris, from which he soon retired, and replaced in Algeria by General Maurice Challe. De Gaulle, through a variety of political and economic measures, endeavored to win the support of Algeria's Muslims, and Challe conducted a vigorous offensive against the FLN that reduced its forces in Algeria by half and forced them to abandon company-size operations and split into small groups.[40] However, because all were not eliminated, there was the danger that, like algae in an aquarium, they would again grow once the pressure against them was relaxed. Moreover, an FLN force of some ten thousand was in being across the border in Tunisia, and there was no assurance that the Morice Line would keep them out forever. Finally, the measures Challe employed turned many farmers and herdsmen into refugees and tended to embitter those who had been displaced.[41]

De Gaulle wanted military success to facilitate reaching a settlement with the FLN under which Algeria, while evolving toward independence, would remain closely associated with France.[42] However, it became clear over time that the FLN would not enter into negotiations until there was a prospect that they would result in bringing French rule to an early end, and on 16 September 1959 de Gaulle announced that the Algerians would be given self-determination.[43] This announcement marked a turning point, opening as it did a widening gap between metropolitan France, where it was favorably received, and Algeria, where extremists and disaffected army officers began to plot a rebellion within the rebellion. In January 1960, in Algiers, Europeans staged a week-long uprising during which many gendarmes were killed and wounded while troops stood by and refused to fire. The uprising was ended by other troops, brought in from operations in the field, whose task was eased by the onset of rain. In the wake of the affair there was another purge of dissident officers, and General Challe, whose inability to control them had lost him the confidence of de Gaulle, was assigned elsewhere a few months later.[44] In December de Gaulle paid a three-day visit to Algeria, which was made the occasion for further rioting in Algiers and for four abortive attempts at de Gaulle's assassination.[45]

In March 1961 de Gaulle and the leaders of the Algerian government-in-exile reached an agreement for peace talks, to be held at Evian, on the shores of Lake Geneva, and this triggered the launching of a military revolt. It began on 22 April, and in Algeria it was led by four five-star generals who had previously served there and had now been smuggled back in: Raoul Salan and Maurice Challe, the former commanders-in-chief, Edmond Jouhaud, who had been born in Algeria and to whom it was home, and Marie-André Zeller, well-known as a firm supporter of *Algérie française*.[46] In metropolitan France they enjoyed the support of a group of conspirators headed by General Jacques Faure, one of the officers who had been purged in the wake of the Algiers uprising of January 1960. Faure and his fellow-conspirators arranged to have bodies of paratroopers hidden in the forests of Orleans and Rambouillet the night of the 22nd, which were to have joined up with tank units to seize key points in the capital. But Faure and other key leaders were arrested before they could arrive on the scene, and the paratroops, not privy to the detailed planning, could only disperse when some gendarmes appeared and ordered them to do so.[47]

In Algiers the plotters quickly seized General Fernand Gambiez, the commander in chief, and General Challe took over responsibility for military affairs. They also took into custody Jean Morin, the government-delegate, Gambiez's civilian opposite number, as well as principal members of his staff, intending that Salan should thenceforth take responsibility for Algeria's governmental affairs. However, Challe, Salan, and the others had no sooner taken charge than things began to go wrong. In France the commander in chief of the air force had proved cooperative in the beginning and there had been enough transports in Algeria to ferry two regiments to France, but he quickly abandoned the rebel cause and pulled almost all the transports back to France. In consequence any thought of invading France had to be abandoned, and an inventory of foodstuffs, medicines, and the funds in the vaults of the Banque de France revealed that an Algeria cut off from the metropole could last little more than a fortnight. In Algeria itself only the commanders in the vicinity of Algiers were proving to be firmly behind the revolt; elsewhere they declared opposition, wavered, or remained noncommittal. On the night of 23 April de Gaulle made a broadcast speech in which he appealed over the heads of rebel commanders to their troops, absolving them of the requirement for obedience. The conspirators having failed to order the jamming of broadcasts from France, tens of thousands of troops heard de Gaulle's speech, and something akin to passive resistance spread among the rank and file. By 26 April—four days and five nights after the putsch had begun—it was clear to the rebels that they had failed. Challe flew back alone to France to give himself up. Jouhaud and Zeller went into hiding, but by the end of the month they and some two hundred other officers were under arrest.[48] Meanwhile another group, headed by Salan, cast their lot with civilian extremists who had formed the Organisation Armée Secrète. Salan and his associates reorganized it along military lines and embarked on a campaign of terrorism in both Algeria and France itself. That campaign—discussed below in the context of its threat to democracy in France—earned the hostility of the people among whom it was conducted and failed to prevent the reaching of an agreement for Algerian independence.[49]

The two successive wars of the third kind fought by France in the wake of World War II also imposed considerable strain upon the people of France, and they in turn brought pressure to bear upon their government, culminating in the threat of civil war.

In this context it is study of the 1954–62 war in Algeria that is the more rewarding. Indochina was a distant land, Algeria was close at hand; few citizens of France lived in Indochina, whereas almost a million had their homes in Algeria; France had much greater military resources to devote to the second of the two conflicts than to that in Indochina, which broke out soon after the liberation of France itself; and the fielding of a larger and more modern army in Algeria involved financial costs of a different order of magnitude.[50] All in all, the Algerian war posed problems on which it was difficult to reach and maintain the consensus essential to government stability under a parliamentary system, with the consequence that six of France's prime ministers fell in the slightly more than three and a half years between the outbreak of that war and de Gaulle's accession to power, and that weeks sometimes elapsed between the fall of one cabinet and the voting into office of another. Finally, consideration of the Algerian war benefits from the fact that it has been the subject of exceptionally fine studies, notably that by Alistair Horne.

It is said that up until 1956, which is to say until the Algerian war had been under way for well over a year, all France was united on the proposition that independence for Algeria was both unthinkable and unmentionable.[51] However, that unity disappeared and the war in Algeria became an increasingly divisive subject as word reached France of the consequences for the people of Algeria of the repeated rakings over of their villages by the French army; of conditions in Algeria's regroupment centers, where there was much suffering and where children, in particular, were reported to be dying in substantial numbers from malnutrition; of horrible mutilations inflicted on dead, wounded, and captive soldiers by some Algerian guerrillas; of shocking atrocities committed by some French soldiers and civilians against Algerians; and, above all, of systematic use of torture during the interrogation of suspects during a period in which paratroopers were in charge of dealing with the campaign of urban violence the FLN unleashed in Algiers early in 1957.[52]

Since the days in which highwaymen had engaged in the practice of holding their victims' feet to the fire, there had been a provision in France's penal code that imposed the death penalty on anyone found guilty of torture.[53] More relevant still, it evoked vividly unpleasant memories of what many French men and women had suffered at the hands of the Gestapo during the 1940–44 Nazi occupation of France. Accounts of French use of torture in Algeria originated from, among others, Paul Teitgen, the secretary-general of Algiers prefecture, who saw on detainees signs of tortures he had himself suffered on numerous occasions some fourteen years earlier, and General Jacques de Bollardière, who had fought during World War II in Norway, at El Alamein, and with the maquis in the Ardennes, as well as in Indochina. After being transferred to Algiers from the field, he had clashed with General Jacques Massu, who was in command of the troops in control of that city, over the use of torture. Later he sent a letter of protest to Jean-Jacques Servan-Schreiber, editor of *L'Express*—who had himself been prosecuted as a "demoralizer" of the war effort for a book based upon his experiences while serving in Algeria. For that breach of discipline, Bollardière was sentenced to sixty days of "fortress arrest."[54]

Thus the Algerian war created serious differences among civilian officials and military officers between those who were determined to end the rebellion by whatever means and those who objected to some of the means being employed. Similar fissures opened in France within the populace as a whole, as well as between the citizenry and officialdom. At the far left was a Marxist group that collected funds for the FLN. On the non-communist left, a group of 121 celebrities signed a declaration on the "right of insubordination" in the Algerian war, which incited conscripts to desert. In the center, the Assembly of French Cardinals and Bishops issued a statement condemning desertion and subversive activities but stressing that orders to engage in torture should be disobeyed. On the right, supporting the cause of maintaining French rule over Algeria, there was the Vincennes Committee headed by Jacques Soustelle, who had been governor-general of Algeria in 1955–56 and Georges Bidault, who had served as provisional president and prime minister in postwar France. In November 1961, after a meeting of the committee at which some of the members praised Salan and the Organisation Armée Secrète, more commonly called the OAS, and during which Bidault talked of a possible coup, de Gaulle ordered the committee dissolved.[55]

In France, the OAS was responsible for acts of terrorism in which hundreds of people were killed or wounded and in which much material damage was done. In April 1961, in response to an announcement that peace talks were about to begin between representatives of the government and of the FLN, and were to take place in the town of Evian, the OAS killed its mayor.[56] That same month the OAS made the first of its dozen or more attempts on the life of de Gaulle. Hiring an ex-legionnaire who proposed to kill de Gaulle with a telescopic rifle, it gave the man a large down payment, only to have him tip off the police and then disappear.[57] During the main offensive of the OAS in France, which it conducted between September 1961 and February of 1962, its terrorists bombed the Quai d'Orsay, the newspapers *France-Soir* and *Figaro,* the apartment of Jean-Paul Sartre, and the home of André Malraux, among their many targets. Neither Sartre nor Malraux was hurt, but at the latter's home a small girl playing with her dolls was partially blinded and badly cut about the face by flying glass, an incident that helped produce a general revulsion against the OAS. The OAS sent threatening letters to many people in an effort to extort funds: Brigitte Bardot received one demanding five million francs and turned it over to *L'Express* with a declaration that she was not going to go along because she did not want to live in "a Nazi country." [58]

In September 1961 the OAS made a spectacular but unsuccessful effort to kill de Gaulle by exploding a mine beside the road as his car passed en route from Paris to his home at Colombey-les-Deux-Églises and in August 1962 an OAS band led by a renegade colonel shot up a car in which de Gaulle and his wife were traveling, but once again the effort failed. [59] His wife having been so endangered, de Gaulle was enraged and ordered an all-out campaign to eliminate the OAS—an objective that was achieved before another year had passed. [60] In the eyes of many, de Gaulle had saved France from civil war. He had also kept the pledge implicit in his answer to a newsman shortly before assuming office. "Is it credible," he had demanded, "that I am going to begin a career as dictator at the age of sixty-seven?" [61]

The Philippine Insurrection, as the first of two wars of the third kind fought by the United States in this century, was a modest affair as compared to the second, the war in Vietnam. The numbers of U.S. troops involved were only about a tenth as large, the conflict was not nearly as long, and it ended in the suppression of the insurrection. In addition, geography tended to limit the one, conducted as it was in an archipelago, and to invite the expansion of the other from the portion of the peninsula on which it had begun. The Philippine Insurrection was, save for a brief initial period, a war between guerrillas and regular troops, whereas the Vietnam War tended, as time went by, to assume the aspect of a conventional war. Nevertheless, each has something to tell us about the bearing of secrecy on the conduct of wars of the third kind and about the relationship between involvement in such conflicts and the health of a democratic polity.

The Philippine Insurrection was fought in circumstances that enabled official Washington to go far toward putting a good face on bad situations, or in hiding them entirely from public view. It was fought in a distant land, where there were virtually no resident Americans, and in a time when the channels through which news could reach the United States were limited to cables and the mail. At home, successive administrations were headed by men—William McKinley, Theodore Roosevelt, and William Howard Taft—whose personal involvement in bringing the Philippines under the American flag came early and whose party and personal ties with one another were exceptionally close. As assistant secretary of the navy during McKinley's first term, Roosevelt had arranged to have Admiral George Dewey's squadron sent to the Far East, in anticipation of war with Spain, with the consequence that it was on hand to destroy the Spanish fleet in Manila Bay within days after the declaration of war. McKinley had made the decision to acquire the archipelago from Spain, and Taft had gone there little more than a year after the insurrection had begun, first as the head of a Philippine Commission and later as the first civilian governor. Roosevelt, succeeding McKinley, appointed Taft to his cabinet as secretary of war, a position that included responsibility for insular affairs. Roosevelt also groomed Taft to succeed him as president. Thus all were inhibited from dealing frankly with the American people in matters any one of them might find embarrassing.

In the early months of the Philippine Insurrection, General Elwell S. Otis, the American commander, sent home a series of overly optimistic reports, which the McKinley administration made available to the press. In Manila Otis's censor, to prevent American correspondents from sending reports that contradicted the picture he was presenting, cut or altered statements of fact on the grounds that "they would alarm the people at home," or "have the people of the United States by the ears." By July 1899 the dozen American correspondents on the scene, unwilling longer to be party to this deception, prepared a joint despatch setting forth the situation as they saw it, and a small group representing the others obtained an interview with Otis. In the course of the interview, a stormy one lasting four hours, he refused to pass the despatch and threatened to "put them off the island." Thereafter they signed the despatch and mailed it to Hong Kong, to be cabled home from there.[62]

In a separate despatch, the representative of the Associated

Press reported having the censor tell him: "My instructions are to let nothing go out that can hurt the administration." In June, the correspondent reported, he had tried to file a despatch saying that reinforcements were needed, only to have the censor confide: "Of course we all know that we are in a terrible mess out here, but we don't want the people to get excited about it. If you fellows will only keep quiet we will pull through in time without any fuss at home." The assumption was that Otis was intent on avoiding embarrassment to McKinley's 1900 campaign for reelection, in which the acquisition of the Philippines was bound to be an issue.[63] But the refusal to pass a despatch expressing the opinion that American troop strength was insufficient suggested that Otis was withholding important information not only from the American people, but from the War Department as well. In 1898 he had estimated that in the event of hostilities, he would need thirty thousand men to occupy the archipelago, and he now stood by that figure despite the fact that his forces were not large enough to garrison the towns he had taken, much less for also conducting offensive operations.[64]

In the United States the publication of the despatches on 17 July 1899 created a great sensation and sharpened public debate between the defenders of the administration's Philippines policy and its critics. They also led to the resignation of Secretary of War Russell A. Alger and his replacement by Elihu Root. On 12 August, at his request, the War Department asked General Otis to report what force he considered would undoubtedly be adequate for the complete suppression of the insurrection during the dry season then approaching. Otis was to consult his general officers before replying, and was told that the secretary, bearing in mind that public impatience might affect legislative provision for the conduct of the war, would prefer to send too many troops rather than too few. Having been urged, Otis admitted that he would need to double his force to sixty thousand men. This figure was only slightly smaller than the total number of men in the regular army, which had been set at a maximum of sixty-five thousand, and to meet Otis's request the War Department issued orders for the enlistment of ten more regiments of volunteers.[65]

After this disastrous affair, Otis supposedly terminated cen-

sorship, but in actuality merely appointed a new censor and became increasingly arbitrary. In Washington, as secretary of war,
Elihu Root acted in much the same spirit, pigeonholing reports
that contained embarrassing information and assuring the public that all complaints coming out of the Philippines were being
made the subject of prompt investigation.[66] However, censorship in Manila and official cover-up in Washington did not prevent the involvement in the Philippines from becoming a bitter
source of contention. Opponents founded and promoted an
Anti-Imperialist League, which eventually had half a million
members, including such well-known figures as ex-presidents
Harrison and Cleveland, Republican Senator George Hoar,
Andrew Carnegie, Jane Addams, John Dewey, and Mark
Twain. Among its activities, it carried on a controversial program designed to discourage young men from enlisting, and its
people found themselves being called "traitors" and "copper-
heads." One of its pamphlets, entitled *The Cost of a National
Crime,* was ordered printed by the Senate as a public document,
but copies sent to regiments being held in the Philippines despite the expiration of their terms of enlistment were removed
from the Philippines pouch in the San Francisco post office.
When this tampering with the mails became known, a further
uproar followed.[67]

Back in the Philippines, the doubling of his force that Otis
had expected to suffice had not enabled him to suppress the insurrection during the dry season to which Root had referred.
Indeed, resistance continued through the remainder of the
McKinley presidency. In the autumn of 1901, when McKinley
was assassinated and Roosevelt succeeded him, the war was still
going on and the American people had become tired of it. In
dealing with that problem, Roosevelt acted in characteristic
fashion: on 4 July 1902 he terminated military rule over the
Philippines and issued a proclamation of peace and amnesty
whereby the insurrection was officially ended.[68]

In some regions, however, resistance still continued, and this
was notably so on the island of Samar. In conducting the pacifi-
cation of Samar, General Jacob Smith had ordered his troops to
kill every Filipino male above the age of ten and to convert the
island into a "howling wilderness."[69] In attempting to carry out

his orders, they destroyed the fabric of social order but did not succeed in ending resistance. By 1904 it became evident that widespread outlawry on Samar called for the institution there of martial law. However, Roosevelt was that year a candidate for reelection, and the institution of martial law was postponed in order not to embarrass his campaign by calling attention to the fact that the insurrection he had declared ended two years earlier was still continuing.[70]

Writing during the administration of President Taft, and from the perspective of one who had served in the Philippines first as an officer of the U.S. Volunteers and then as a U.S. district judge, James E. Blount declared: "No administration has ever yet during the last fourteen years been in a position to be frank with the Senate and the country concerning the situation at any given time in the Philippines, because at any given time there was always so much that it could not afford to reopen and explain."[71] Conceding that Elihu Root had been an extraordinarily effective secretary of war, Blount nevertheless observed: "The splendor of Mr. Root's intellect is positively alluring, but he is a dangerous man for republican institutions . . . because he is of the type who are constantly finding situations they consider it best for people not to know about."[72] All of the men concerned, he conceded, "were personally men of high type." Nevertheless, he continued, "loyalty to the original ill-considered decision became impregnated, in their case, with a fervor not entirely unlike religious fanaticism, and belief in it became a matter of principle, justifying all they had done, and guiding all they might thereafter do."[73]

In March 1968 President Lyndon B. Johnson, in his quest for victory in Vietnam, found himself at a dead end. General Westmoreland had asked to have another two hundred thousand men sent to reinforce the half million already there. However, the generals in the Pentagon could give the secretary of defense no assurance that the additional troops—or, indeed, any particular number—would suffice to bring the struggle in Vietnam to a successful conclusion. Nevertheless, General Earle G. Wheeler, the chairman of the Joint Chiefs of Staff, had rejected suggestions for a change of strategy. Both he and General Maxwell D. Taylor, his predecessor and now a White House consultant, were urging the politically unpalatable measure of calling up the reserves. In his perplexity President Johnson sought the counsels of members of his Senior Informal Advisory Council, more commonly known as the Wise Men. Most of these men, almost all of them former incumbents of high position who were no longer in office, had until then been supporters of the government's Vietnam policy. But now, against the background of their own recognition of the extent to which the Vietnam involvement was opening divisions within American society and on the basis of a series of official briefings and discussions among themselves, almost all felt that some action had to be taken to reduce the American involvement and to find a way out.[74] This was the context, it may be remembered, of President Johnson's announced decisions of 31 March 1968 to deescalate the bombing of North Vietnam, to move toward peace through negotiations, and to leave office at the end of his term rather than to seek reelection.[75]

About two and a half years after leaving office—at a time when antiwar demonstrations in the United States were at their height—Lyndon Johnson was described as feeling that failure to impose censorship had been a mistake.[76] In 1979, four years after the war in Vietnam had ended, a similar remark was attributed to Dean Rusk, who had perhaps been Johnson's closest advisor. "If another war like Vietnam comes up," he is reported to have said, "the leaders and the Congress should take a hard look at censorship, such as we had in World War II."[77] However, neither was quoted as explaining what course of action he believed the United States could have pursued to a successful conclusion but for the failure to institute censorship.

Upon assuming office as secretary of defense, a few weeks before President Johnson announced his decision not to run again, Clark Clifford asked his military advisers whether the war could be ended by the continuing bombing of North Vietnam. They replied that, by itself, it could not: the United States had already dropped a heavier tonnage of bombs there than in all theaters during World War II. He then asked what plan there was for achieving victory, and was told there was none. There was none because the president had forbidden them to invade

North Vietnam lest the Chinese intervene or to pursue the enemy into Laos and Cambodia, because to do so would widen the war geographically and politically.[78]

The People's Republic of China had responded to the U.S. buildup in Vietnam of half a million men, and to the campaign of bombing against North Vietnam, with a series of measures that included sending fifty thousand troops of the People's Liberation Army into North Vietnam. As a token of readiness to engage the United States, should it attempt to conquer North Vietnam, this buildup was a reminder of the Chinese entry into the Korean War that had followed upon the approach of U.S. forces to China's border with North Korea.[79] As Lyndon Johnson's successor in the presidency, Richard Nixon proved no more anxious to carry the ground war to North Vietnam than his predecessor. However, he did carry the war to Cambodia, insofar as possible under conditions of secrecy that censorship could hardly have improved upon, and to Laos as well.

In keeping with President Nixon's Vietnamization policy, U.S. troops were to be withdrawn as South Vietnamese forces gained the capability to take their place. In the event, it proved not to be practicable to keep U.S. forces in Vietnam as long as that would have required. Indeed, it may have been realized at the start that this would be so, and in the interest of improving the prospects of Vietnamization, the United States quickly began extending the war to Cambodia.

On 15 March 1969 President Nixon authorized the Joint Chiefs of Staff to begin the bombing by B-52 aircraft of twelve areas of Cambodia neighboring South Vietnam that had been identified as sanctuaries for Viet Cong and North Vietnamese troops.[80] In order to keep knowledge of this bombing campaign from the people, the press, and the Congress, a dual reporting system was put into effect. The usual system of reporting to the command and control system of the Strategic Air Command was continued, but with the raids falsely reported as having been conducted against objectives in Vietnam. It was only in the second and highly secret set of reports that the true targets were given. Some officers were upset about the requirement to submit false reports, which was a court martial offense, but it was not until four years later that one of them was to reveal the secret by writing a congressional committee to complain.[81]

On 9 May 1969 the *New York Times* carried a report by William Beecher on the first of the raids on Cambodia. He had produced the report on the basis of stray bits of information, picked up in the Pentagon and at the White House, and evaluated against a background of personal knowledge that there were no targets of consequence in the area of Vietnam that supposedly had been bombed. The report failed to arouse public or congressional interest, but in the White House it gave rise to misapprehensions that someone had been guilty of a deliberate leak. In the hope of identifying the culprit, wiretaps were placed on the phones of three members of the White House staff, seven members of the staff of the National Security Council, and a number of newsmen, and were kept in place for periods of upward of two years.[82]

In the spring of 1970, despite the U.S. bombing campaign, which had been conducted for almost a year, North Vietnamese and Viet Cong forces remained across the border in Cambodia and within striking distance of Saigon. It was considered unsafe, in the circumstances, to continue the withdrawal of U.S. troops from Vietnam, and in April U.S. and South Vietnamese troops mounted spoiling operations against the occupants of the sanctuaries, operations they pushed in as far as the Cambodian capital of Phnom Penh. The invading forces inflicted thousands of casualties and captured enormous quantities of weapons and supplies; they also brought the ground war and disaster to Cambodia. Its leader Lon Nol, not realizing that U.S. forces were not to remain beyond the end of June, made it known to the Vietnamese Communists that their use of Cambodian sanctuaries would no longer be tolerated.[83] The North Vietnamese and the Viet Cong, in need of all the help they could get, made common cause with the Khmer Rouge—Cambodian communist guerrillas with whom they had until then had a relationship characterized by mutual suspicion. Fighting soon spread throughout the Cambodian countryside, and in June General Abrams cabled the Joint Chiefs of Staff that Vietnamization would have to be slowed down and South Vietnamese forces allowed to remain in Cambodia for some weeks longer than intended to prevent that country from falling to the Communists. In Washington, Secretary of Defense Melvin Laird complained that South Vietnamese troops were wandering all over Cambodia protecting that country while U.S. troops in turn were in South Vietnam protecting the Vietnamese.[84] Indeed, as late as September there were twenty-one battalions of South Vietnamese troops in Cambodia, and a major part of the South Vietnamese air force was committed to their support.[85]

In the United States the invasion of Cambodia, undertaken without consultation with the Congress and coming as a surprise to the American people, set off antiwar protests across the country. Students on the campuses were in an uproar, and after a number of them were killed and wounded by National Guardsmen at Kent State University, a huge antiwar demonstration was staged in Washington itself. President Nixon would not believe that the antiwar demonstrations were wholly spontaneous and called upon his intelligence people to uncover the agents of Communist countries who must be responsible.[86] Nixon also approved a plan by Thomas Charles Huston, a member of the White House staff, under which the intelligence agencies of the federal government would have resorted to mail intercepts, burglaries, and other illegal measures, but it was not put into effect because of the objections of FBI director J. Edgar Hoover and Attorney General John N. Mitchell.[87]

In February 1971, there having been another North Vietnamese and Viet Cong supply buildup across South Vietnam's border, this time in Laos, another cross-border operation was mounted. It was conducted by two South Vietnamese divisions with U.S. air support. As a spoiling operation it achieved a modicum of success, but at the cost of a South Vietnamese casualty rate of nearly 50 percent. During this operation American pilots flew 160,000 sorties, during which 107 helicopters were lost to enemy fire, a loss rate of 60 percent.[88] In a television speech of 7 April, President Nixon described the performance of the participating South Vietnamese forces as evidence that Vietnamization had succeeded. However, the invasion of Laos was attended by a renewal of public protests, often with returned veterans in the lead, and in the latter part of April some two hundred thousand protesters took part in one of Washington's biggest antiwar rallies.[89]

On 13 June the *New York Times* began the publication of the *Pentagon Papers*. Though the study's seven thousand pages of secret documents related to the conduct of the war during the Johnson administration, President Nixon and his aides saw its publication as a security breach that might be followed by the revelation of secrets of their own that they were anxious to protect, and as itself an act of protest against the war. Morton Halperin, who had served on the National Security Council in the early years of the Nixon administration, and Leslie H. Gelb, a former director of the Pentagon's policy planning staff, were reported to be working at the Brookings Institution on a study of the Vietnam War, assertedly with the benefit of government documents that they had retained upon leaving office, and there was no telling what secrets they might reveal.[90]

Such was the background for the creation in the White House itself of the Special Investigations Unit, more commonly referred to as "the plumbers" because its primary task was to be the stopping of leaks, which intended to use means that included those contemplated under the discarded Huston plan of the previous year. Nixon wanted the files of Gelb and Halperin to be retrieved and brought to the White House. A little earlier the plumbers had made a successful break-in at the office of a psychiatrist in search of confidential information that might be used, it was hoped, in efforts to discredit Daniel Ellsberg. Now a plan was worked out under which the Brookings Institution was to be firebombed and the papers retrieved during the resultant confusion. This plan was rejected as too risky, and no alternative was put into effect while the plumbers were still in business. It was, of course, the bungled break-in at the headquarters of the Democratic National Committee, as a fouling of the well of American electoral politics, that was their and Nixon's undoing. Nevertheless, H. R. Haldeman was undoubtedly correct when he declared that the Vietnam War "destroyed Nixon as completely as it shattered President Johnson."[91]

The foregoing examples illustrate the validity of assertions advanced at the beginning of this chapter: that inability to bring wars of the third kind to a successful conclusion is likely to cause the leaders of great powers to extend their geographic scope and thus to enlarge the wars themselves; that such wars, especially when so extended, can lead to military disaster; and that they can undermine the state polities of countries that embark upon them. In the example of Japan, the military having suppressed all civilian dissent, extension of the war ended both in military defeat and in the destruction of their regime. During the Algerian war for independence, the extension of hostilities to Egypt proved to be an embarrassing mistake, while the long and unsuccessful effort to hold Algeria destroyed the Fourth Republic and endangered the Fifth Republic that succeeded it. The Philippine Insurrection demonstrated that even a relatively short war of the third kind can create bitter divisions within the country that carries it on, and that censorship can deprive a government itself of important information. Finally, the danger to constitutional rule, seen as flowing from the governmental secrecy that attended counterinsurgency in the Philippines, emerged unmistakably during the latter years of the Vietnam War. It was that secrecy, or more particularly the methods used in efforts to maintain it, that led the House Judiciary Committee to pass against Richard Nixon three articles of impeachment, in one of which he was charged with abusing his power and repeatedly violating the rights of citizens, rights set forth in the Constitution he had sworn to uphold and defend.[92]

7 Reflections

The U.S. experience in Vietnam is now more than two decades in the past, and it is appropriate to ask what wisdom has been drawn from it by the military, their political masters, the scholarly community, and the populace at large. In the Introduction, I cited a conference that had the Vietnam War as its subject during which the eminent political scientist Samuel P. Huntington declared: "It is conceivable that our policy-makers may best meet future crises and dilemmas if they simply blot out of their minds any recollection of this one." The situational characteristics of that entanglement were in many respects unique, he pointed out, and it was likely that any lessons drawn from it would be the wrong ones. This prompted his Harvard colleague John Kenneth Galbraith to write that Huntington was, in effect, urging that we must not allow our Vietnam experience to weaken our will to intervene for a similar result somewhere else.[1]

However well-taken Galbraith's comment, Huntington's observation about wrong lessons was not without point. Thus, as we have already noted, Dean Rusk—secretary of state throughout the presidencies of John F. Kennedy and Lyndon B. Johnson—drew the conclusion that the leaders and the Congress should, if another such war came up, take a hard look at instituting censorship. Similarly, General Maxwell D. Taylor, who had held such high posts as chairman of the Joint Chiefs of Staff and ambassador to Saigon during those same presidencies, later held that any future president, in deciding upon another intervention like Vietnam, would be well advised to seek a declaration of war or of emergency in order "to silence future critics by exercising executive order."[2] However, neither Rusk nor Taylor seems to have explained what measures—measures that might have made it possible to bring the Vietnam War to a victorious conclusion—were foreclosed by the failure to impose censorship or suppress dissent. In fact, it was efforts to suppress dissent that brought on Watergate and destroyed the presidency of Richard M. Nixon.[3]

It may be recalled that Hans Morgenthau, as recounted in the Introduction, took issue with Huntington's assertion that, because the situational characteristics of our Vietnam entanglement were unique, it might be best to draw no conclusions from it. It was no new discovery, Morgenthau observed, that historical phenomena are unique in one sense, but it was obvious also that they are in another sense typical. If they were only unique, he concluded, historical phenomena would merely be oddities from which nothing could be learned. Indeed, as Richard E. Neustadt and Ernest R. May have pointed out, decision makers facing current problems can often find useful guidance from analogous cases drawn from the past provided they identify and strip away the dissimilarities.[4]

The potentially most useful analogy available to the Kennedy and Johnson administrations, in deciding whether to deepen U.S. involvement in Indochina, was the immediately preceding experience there of France. The theater of operations, the enemy, the cause, and the kind of war were all the same. But the analogy seems to have been accepted as valid by nobody in the upper ranks of the government except Undersecretary of State George W. Ball. On the basis of close connections of many years' standing with numbers of high French leaders, Ball had gained an understanding of the kind of conflict in which France had been engaged, not only in Southeast Asia following the end of World War II, but again in Algeria between 1954 and 1962.[5]

Ball's colleagues, however, saw France's difficulties as arising in large part from its status as a colonial power trying to keep another people in subjection, and from the militarily weak state in which it had emerged from World War II. At the same time they saw the United States as having no designs on South Vietnam save that of backing its independence, without adequately examining the presumption that the Vietnamese, in spite of our recent support of the French, would not see us in the same light. Moreover, Ball's colleagues, while correct in seeing the United States as a military power of a wholly different order to post–World War II France, overestimated the roles in such a war of sophisticated weapons and weight of ordnance. They preferred the analogy of the Korean War to that of the French experience in Vietnam, partly because they were acquainted with it, and partly because it was more reassuring. They also did not adequately take into account the basic difference that one was a conventional war and the other was not.[6]

The Kennedy and Johnson administrations would have been better served had their leaders been able, as the reader is by now, to distinguish clearly between conventional warfare and wars of the third kind, and to draw upon a body of relevant generalizations rather than a single analogy—and an ill-chosen one at that—as many of them did.

In justice to those leaders, one must recognize that they had inherited from the Eisenhower administration a commitment from which it would be difficult to disengage. That administration, in the wake of the French defeat and the partition of Vietnam into the communist North and the non-communist South, had pledged full U.S. support to Ngo Dinh Diem, the prime minister of South Vietnam. It had undertaken the training of South Vietnam's armed forces, extended to it other forms of assistance, and led in the formation of a Southeast Asia Treaty Organization intended to protect the country not only against armed attack, but against other threats to its security as well.[7] During this period President Eisenhower, recalling that Republican orators had since 1949 been taxing the Democrats with having "lost China," told his cabinet that he could not afford to give the Democrats a basis for asking, "Who lost Vietnam?"[8] That was a question the Democrats, once burned, were twice careful, after they came to power, to avoid—as Lyndon B.

Johnson was subsequently to admit.[9] In consequence, ironically, it was to the Republican administration of Richard M. Nixon that the task of disengaging the United States from the war in South Vietnam finally fell.

Against the background of what might be called a proxy war against Nicaragua's Sandinistas, there has in recent times been talk within the Reagan administration of an actual U.S. invasion of that country. Early in 1987 General Paul Gorman, commander of U.S. forces in the region, told the Senate Armed Services Committee: "You're not going to knock off the Sandinistas with a conventional armed force, and that's what the Contras are."[10] Gorman was in a position to speak candidly because he was retiring from the army, but he was not alone in that assessment of the Contras.

It was evidently against the background of a similar estimate that Lieutenant Colonel Oliver L. North of the National Security Council staff reportedly proposed a plan that would have provided the pretext for a U.S. invasion of Nicaragua. Under this plan, the contras would have been ordered to seize and try to hold a town in Nicaragua, anticipating that they would soon find themselves in danger of annihilation and that their plight would arouse American sympathies sufficient to permit the sending in of a U.S. rescuing force. Assistant Secretary of State for Inter-American Affairs Elliott Abrams, testifying to this effect on 2 June 1987 at the congressional hearings on the Iran-Contra affair, had thought this an interesting idea, and it doubtless would have been viewed with approval by others who were asserting that invading Nicaragua would be "like falling off a log," and could be accomplished in four to six weeks.[11]

The case against a U.S. invasion of Nicaragua had been persuasively set forth in June 1985, on the eve of his retirement, by General Wallace H. Nutting, then commander of the Readiness Command, the force that would be employed in carrying it out. Doubtless remembering that the U.S. marines had tried in vain, from 1927 to 1933, to suppress the insurrection led by Augusto Sandino, despite the assistance of the U.S.-trained Nicaraguan National Guard, General Nutting declared that an invasion of Nicaragua would require a major operation, and that the occupation of the country would not mark the end of the struggle. Moreover, it would cost us dear in our relations with other Latin American countries and be a source of dissension with our NATO allies. "Instead of worrying about invading Nicaragua," he was quoted as saying, "we should be concentrating on developing the hemispheric idea of a coalition, building strength through political reform and economic development in the surrounding countries." With insurgencies under way in El Salvador and Guatemala, he granted the need for a minimum of military assistance to restore public order and provide security. However, he went on, "in this case, smaller is better; the less visible we are militarily, the better it will be." [12]

General Nutting's opposition to a U.S. invasion of Nicaragua was widely shared among senior military officers, but not necessarily for reasons that would ensure against another Vietnam. Writing in 1986 from the perspectives of a recent teaching assignment at West Point, followed by service in the Strategic Plans and Policy Division of the army staff, Major Andrew F. Krepinevich, Jr., reported that there had been a resurgence of interest among the military in what is now referred to as low-intensity warfare. The army, he wrote, would resist being drawn into another war like Vietnam unless certain conditions existed. As drawn up by such people as a recent army chief of staff and an Army War College strategist, and enunciated by Secretary of Defense Caspar W. Weinberger, these conditions included the existence of an atmosphere of public and congressional support, a readiness to commit troops sufficient for the accomplishment of their mission, and a "clear intention of winning" on the part of the country's political leadership. This latter condition, Krepinevich wrote, represented a built-in excuse for failure: should the military become frustrated in such a war in the future, "being allowed to win" would mean freedom to escalate the conflict to the more congenial environment of conventional war. As though echoing Huntington's assertion, Krepinevich remarked that "if the army has learned any lessons from Vietnam, it has learned many of the wrong ones." [13]

An escalation to the environment of conventional war implies the geographic extension of the conflict from the scene in which a war of the third kind is taking place and an attack on the real or presumed source of the support believed to enable the enemy to maintain his struggle. Such an extension is likely to add to the problems of those who undertake it, as we have seen in the cases of the extension of France's war in Algeria to Egypt, that by the United States from Vietnam to Cambodia, and—most disastrously of all cases that come to mind—the successive extensions of Japan's North China adventure to East and South China, from South China to Indochina, and finally to Pearl Harbor.

The geographic extension of a conflict, accompanied by its elevation to the environment of conventional warfare, is most apt to be undertaken in an atmosphere of great frustration by officials whose long preoccupation with the problems they face inevitably distorts their perspective, and whose commitment to the course upon which they are set is so great as to make the thought of turning back—with its implicit admission of error—painful in the extreme.

In the case of World War II Japan, as we have seen, censorship of the press and the concentration of power in the hands of the military were such that effective opposition was impossible. The only leaders who retained perspective seem to have been civilians, foremost among them the emperor. The emperor reigned but did not rule, however, and the military were able to override his objections. In the case of U.S. involvement in Vietnam, freedom of the press and the right of dissent were available to provide a different perspective and to force it upon the attention of officialdom. As Assistant Secretary of Defense John T. McNaughton wrote in May 1967: "A feeling is widely and strongly held that the Establishment is out of its mind, and that we are carrying things to absurd lengths."[14]

We might now return to the question, posed at the beginning of this chapter, of how much wisdom has been gained in the decades just past concerning wars of the third kind. It would seem that the scholarly community has reached no consensus on the lessons of Vietnam, and the current political leadership of the country gives scant evidence of having considered them at all. The leaders of the defense establishment reflect, as they should, the reluctance which exists within the military services to contemplate another experience like Vietnam. However, in attributing the outcome there to inadequate public and congressional support, unreadiness to commit enough troops, and lack of a clear intention to win on the part of responsible officials, those leaders demonstrate a seriously deficient understanding of wars of the third kind.

One might wish that both the political and the military leaders of the country, when contemplating military interventions in countries of the Third World, would ponder the warning of 1 Corinthians: "But God hath chosen the foolish things of the world to confound the wise; and God hath chosen the weak things of the world to confound the things which are mighty" (1 Cor. 1:27).

Notes

Introduction

1. Russell F. Weigley, *The American Way of War: A History of United States Military Strategy and Policy* (New York: Macmillan, 1973), p. 457.
2. Douglas S. Blaufarb, *The Counterinsurgency Era: U.S. Doctrine and Performance, 1950 to the Present* (New York: Free Press, 1977), p. 80.
3. Richard M. Pfeffer, ed., *No More Vietnams? The War and the Future of American Foreign Policy* (New York: Harper & Row, 1968), pp. 11, 13.
4. Dean Acheson, *Present at the Creation: My Years in the State Department* (New York: W. W. Norton, 1969), pp. 346–48.
5. *The China White Paper: August 1949* (Stanford: Stanford University Press, 1967), p. 311.
6. Ibid., pp. 339–46, 354, 356, 353.
7. Ibid., p. 768.
8. Ibid., p. 262.
9. Ibid., p. 814.
10. Tang Tsou, *America's Failure in China, 1941–50* (Chicago: University of Chicago Press, 1963), pp. 458–59.
11. David Halberstam, *The Best and the Brightest* (New York: Random House, 1972), p. 163.
12. *Foreign Relations of the United States, 1950: East Asia and Pacific* (Washington, D.C.: Department of State, 1978), pp. 1433–38.

13. Blaufarb, *Counterinsurgency Era,* pp. 62–69, 74.
14. Ibid., pp. 80, 259–60.
15. *The Pentagon Papers* (New York: Bantam Books, 1971), pp. 120–21.
16. Ibid., p. 125.
17. Roger Hilsman, *To Move a Nation: The Politics of Foreign Policy in the Administration of John F. Kennedy* (Garden City, N.Y.: Doubleday, 1967), pp. 310–19, and my own recollections.
18. Pfeffer, *No More Vietnams?* pp. 1–3.

Chapter 1

1. Hugh Thomas, *Cuba: The Pursuit of Freedom* (New York: Harper & Row, 1971), 233–41.
2. Ibid., pp. 241–42, 246.
3. Ibid., pp. 248–49.
4. Ibid., p. 259.
5. W. F. Johnson, *The History of Cuba* (New York: B. F. Buck, 1920), III: 287–88.
6. James Hyde Clark, *Cuba and the Fight for Freedom* (Philadelphia: Globe, 1896), p. 322; Thomas, *Cuba,* pp. 265–67.
7. Thomas, *Cuba,* pp. 269, 279.
8. Ibid., pp. 316–20.
9. Ibid., p. 453.
10. Thomas E. Skidmore and Peter H. Smith, *Modern Latin America* (New York: Oxford University Press, 1984), pp. 258–62.
11. Ramiro Guerra y Sánchez, *Sugar and Society in the Caribbean: An Economic History of Cuban Agriculture* (New Haven: Yale University Press, 1964), pp. xxix–xxxii, 86.
12. Robert F. Smith, *The United States and Cuba: Business and Diplomacy, 1917–1960* (New York: Bookman, 1960), p. 229 n. 64, citing R. Hart Phillips, *Cuba: Island of Paradox* (New York: Astor-Honor, 1960), p. 127.
13. Thomas, *Cuba,* pp. 574, 581, 587, 607.
14. Ibid., pp. 591–92, 594.
15. Ibid., pp. 594–96, 606–6.
16. Ibid., p. 608.
17. Ibid., pp. 608–14.
18. Ibid., pp. 615–25.
19. Ibid., p. 625.
20. Ibid., p. 549.

21. Ibid., p. 629.
22. Ibid., pp. 627–28.
23. Ibid., pp. 582–83.
24. Ibid., pp. 634, 637.
25. Skidmore and Smith, *Modern Latin America,* p. 264; Thomas, *Cuba,* pp. 634–35, 638–39.
26. Thomas, *Cuba,* pp. 645–49.
27. Philip F. Dur, "Conditions for Recognition," *Foreign Service Journal,* September 1985, p. 44.
28. Thomas, *Cuba,* p. 655.
29. Ibid., pp. 645, 648.
30. Ibid., pp. 671–72.
31. Dur, "Conditions for Recognition," pp. 44–45.
32. Ibid., p. 45.
33. Ibid., pp. 44–46; Smith, *United States and Cuba,* p. 155.
34. Dur, "Conditions for Recognition," p. 46.
35. Thomas, *Cuba,* pp. 694–95.
36. Ibid., pp. 695–96.
37. Walter LaFeber, *Inevitable Revolutions: The United States in Central America* (New York: W. W. Norton, 1983), pp. 142–43.
38. Skidmore and Smith, *Modern Latin America,* pp. 268–69.
39. Stephen E. Ambrose, *Eisenhower: The President* (New York: Simon & Schuster, 1984), p. 505.
40. John Weeks, *The Economics of Central America* (New York: Holmes & Meier, 1985), pp. 153–54; Shirley Christian, *Nicaragua: Revolution in the Family* (New York: Random House, 1985), p. 5.
41. Neill Macaulay, *The Sandino Affair* (Durham: Duke University Press), pp. 24–25.
42. Ibid., p. 32; LaFeber, *Inevitable Revolutions,* p. 65.
43. Christian, *Nicaragua,* pp. 8–9; LaFeber, *Inevitable Revolutions,* p. 65.
44. LaFeber, *Inevitable Revolutions,* p. 65.
45. Ibid., pp. 66–67.
46. Ibid., p. 67.
47. Ibid., pp. 67–68; Anderson, *Politics in Central America,* p. 151; Willard L. Beaulac, "Nicaragua," *Foreign Service Journal,* February 1980, p. 13.
48. Christian, *Nicaragua,* p. 19.
49. Ibid., pp. 19–20; Anderson, *Politics in Central America,* p. 151.
50. Beaulac, "Nicaragua," pp. 13–14; Macaulay, *The Sandino Affair,* pp. 251–56.
51. Macaulay, *Sandino Affair,* pp. 254–56.

52. Anderson, *Politics in Central America,* p. 151.

53. LaFeber, *Inevitable Revolutions,* p. 69.

54. Christian, *Nicaragua,* p. 21.

55. LaFeber, *Inevitable Revolutions,* pp. 160–63; Penny Lernoux, *Cry of the People: United States Involvement in the Rise of Fascism, Torture, and Murder, and the Persecution of the Catholic Church in Latin America* (New York: Doubleday, 1980), p. 82.

56. Anderson, *Politics in Central America,* pp. 149–50.

57. LaFeber, *Inevitable Revolutions,* pp. 160, 229.

58. Christian, *Nicaragua,* p. 24.

59. Anderson, *Politics in Central America,* pp. 151–52.

60. Christian, *Nicaragua,* pp. 35, 106.

61. LaFeber, *Inevitable Revolutions,* pp. 108–9, 162–63, 233.

62. *Encyclopedia Britannica,* 1959 ed., s.v. "Costa Rica."

63. Thomas P. Anderson, *Matanza: El Salvador's Communist Revolt of 1932* (Lincoln: University of Nebraska Press, 1971), pp. 38–39; Macaulay, *Sandino Affair,* p. 157.

64. Christian, *Nicaragua,* p. 27.

65. Ibid., pp. 27–30; Anderson, *Politics in Central America,* pp. 153–154.

66. Christian, *Nicaragua,* p. 30; Anderson, *Politics in Central America,* p. 153; Omar Cabezas, *Fire from the Mountain: The Making of a Sandinista* (New York: Crown, 1985), pp. 13–17.

67. LaFeber, *Inevitable Revolutions,* pp. 226–28; Christian, *Nicaragua,* p. 30; Anderson, *Politics in Latin America,* p. 155; Weeks, *Economics of Central America,* p. 155.

68. LaFeber, *Inevitable Revolutions,* p. 228.

69. Ibid., pp. 228–29; Christian, *Nicaragua,* pp. 31–32.

70. Christian, *Nicaragua,* p. 32; LaFeber, *Inevitable Revolutions,* p. 229.

71. Christian, *Nicaragua,* pp. 32–33.

72. Ibid., pp. 28, 51–52, 80; Beaulac, "Nicaragua," p. 15.

73. Anderson, *Politics in Latin America,* pp. 157–58; Christian, *Nicaragua,* pp. 46–49.

74. Christian, *Nicaragua,* pp. 46–50.

75. Ibid., pp. 25, 46–51.

76. Ibid., p. 51.

77. Ibid., pp. 60–65; Anderson, *Politics in Latin America,* pp. 158–59.

78. Christian, *Nicaragua,* pp. 66–67.

79. Ibid., pp. 82–83.

80. Ibid., p. 48.

81. Ibid., p. 60.

82. Ibid., pp. 88–89.

83. Stephen Schlesinger and Stephen Kinzer, *Bitter Fruit: The Untold Story of the American Coup in Guatemala* (Garden City, N.Y.: Doubleday, 1982), pp. 25–31.

84. Ibid., pp. 25–35.

85. Ibid., pp. 49–50.

86. Ibid., pp. 52–53.

87. Anderson, *Politics in Central America,* p. 22.

88. Schlesinger and Kinzer, *Bitter Fruit,* p. 53.

89. LaFeber, *Inevitable Revolutions,* p. 118.

90. Ibid., pp. 75, 118.

91. Schlesinger and Kinzer, *Bitter Fruit,* pp. 70–72.

92. Blanche Wiesen Cook, *The Declassified Eisenhower: A Divided Legacy* (Garden City, N.Y.: Doubleday, 1982), pp. 376–77 n. 11.

93. Schlesinger and Kinzer, *Bitter Fruit,* p. 76.

94. LaFeber, *Inevitable Revolutions,* pp. 116–17.

95. Schlesinger and Kinzer, *Bitter Fruit,* pp. 79–91.

96. Ibid., p. 95.

97. Ibid., p. 92.

98. Ibid., pp. 58–63; LaFeber, *Inevitable Revolutions,* p. 117; Cook, *Declassified Eisenhower,* p. 234.

99. Anderson, *Politics in Central America,* p. 22; Schlesinger and Kinzer, *Bitter Fruit,* p. 70; LaFeber, *Inevitable Revolutions,* p. 118.

100. Cook, *Declassified Eisenhower,* p. 228.

101. Schlesinger and Kinzer, *Bitter Fruit,* pp. 100–101.

102. Ambrose, *Eisenhower,* p. 192; Cook, *Declassified Eisenhower,* p. 282.

103. Cook, *Declassified Eisenhower,* pp. 263–72, 278.

104. Schlesinger and Kinzer, *Bitter Fruit,* p. 120.

105. Cook, *Declassified Eisenhower,* pp. 239–40.

106. Schlesinger and Kinzer, *Bitter Fruit,* pp. 115–16.

107. Ibid., p. 115.

108. Ibid., pp. 170–71; Cook, *Declassified Eisenhower,* p. 228.

109. LaFeber, *Inevitable Revolutions,* p. 124; Schlesinger and Kinzer, *Bitter Fruit,* pp. 171–72.

110. Schlesinger and Kinzer, *Bitter Fruit,* pp. 179–82.

111. Ambrose, *Eisenhower,* p. 195.

112. Schlesinger and Kinzer, *Bitter Fruit,* pp. 186–87.

113. Ibid., p. 183.

114. Ibid., pp. 191–201.

115. Ibid., pp. 208–12.

116. Cook, *Declassified Eisenhower,* p. 286.

117. Schlesinger and Kinzer, *Bitter Fruit,* pp. 218–19, 221.
118. Anderson, *Politics in Central America,* p. 23.
119. Ibid.; Cook, *Declassified Eisenhower,* p. 387; LaFeber, *Inevitable Revolutions,* p. 125; Schlesinger and Kinzer, *Bitter Fruit,* p. 221.
120. Anderson, *Politics in Central America,* pp. 23–24; Schlesinger and Kinzer, *Bitter Fruit,* p. 238.
121. Schlesinger and Kinzer, *Bitter Fruit,* pp. 238–39.
122. Ibid., pp. 239–41.
123. Ibid., pp. 245–56.
124. Ibid., pp. 249–53; Anderson, *Politics in Latin America,* pp. 25–27, 55.
125. Stephen Kinzer, "Walking the Tightrope in Guatemala: A Civilian President Balances Reform and Rightist Pressures," *New York Times Magazine,* 9 November 1986; *New York Times,* 18 March 1985.
126. Schlesinger and Kinzer, *Bitter Fruit,* pp. 247–51; LaFeber, *Inevitable Revolutions,* p. 257; Skidmore and Smith, *Modern Latin America,* p. 319.
127. Lars Schöultz, "Guatemala: Social Change and Political Conflict," in *Trouble in Our Backyard: Central America in the Eighties,* ed. Martin Diskin (New York: Pantheon Books, 1983), p. 188; Anderson, *Politics in Central America,* p. 38.
128. "Notes and Comment," *New Yorker,* 29 July 1985, p. 20.
129. Stephen Kinzer, "Walking the Tightrope in Guatemala."
130. Schlesinger and Kinzer, *Bitter Fruit,* p. 229.
131. Ibid., p. 254; Stephen Kinzer, "Walking the Tightrope in Guatemala."
132. Stephen Kinzer, "Walking the Tightrope in Guatemala."
133. *New York Times,* 3 November 1986.
134. Stephen Kinzer, "Walking the Tightrope in Guatemala."

Chapter 2

1. J. F. A. Lemière de Corvey, "Un Peu de fanatisme," in *The Guerrilla Reader: A Historical Anthology,* ed. Walter Laqueur (Philadelphia: Temple University Press, 1977), p. 64.
2. Edward E. Rice, *Mao's Way* (Berkeley and Los Angeles: University of California Press, 1972), pp. 237–39.
3. John F. Baddeley, *The Russian Conquest of the Caucasus* (London: Longmans, Green, 1908), p. 112; Lesley Blanch, *The Sabres of Paradise* (London: John Murray, 1960), pp. 299–301, 390–91.
4. Mao Zedong, *Selected Works* (Beijing: Foreign Languages Press, 1965), I: 124–25.
5. Baddeley, *Russian Conquest,* p. 117.

6. Mao, *Selected Works*, I: 64–65.

7. Charles C. Cumberland, *The Mexican Revolution: The Constitutionalist Years* (Austin: University of Texas Press, 1972), pp. 194–97; Robert E. Quirk, *The Mexican Revolution, 1914–1915* (New York: Norton, 1960), pp. 184–85.

8. Luis Taruc, *Born of the People* (New York: International Publishers, 1953), p. 169.

9. William W. Whitson, *The Chinese High Command: A History of Communist Military Politics, 1927–71* (New York: Praeger, 1973), p. 353; O. Edmund Clubb, *20th Century China* (New York: Columbia University Press, 1978), p. 291.

10. Abraham Guillen, "Urban Guerrilla Strategy," in *Guerrilla Reader,* ed. Laqueur, pp. 229–37.

11. Douglas Pike, *Viet Cong: The Organization and Techniques of the National Liberation Front of South Vietnam* (Cambridge, Mass.: MIT Press, 1966), p. 251.

Chapter 3

1. Michael Lindsay, *The Unknown War: North China 1937–1945* (London: Bergstrom & Boyle, 1975), p. 82.

2. Mark Mayo Boatner III, *Encyclopedia of the American Revolution* (New York: David McKay, 1974), pp. 528, 1163.

3. Walter Laqueur, *Guerrilla: A Historical and Critical Study* (London: Weidenfeld & Nicholson, 1977), p. 31.

4. Lemière de Corvey, "Un Peu de fanatisme," in *Guerrilla Reader,* ed. Laqueur, p. 65.

5. Ibid., p. 64.

6. Karl Marx and Friedrich Engels, "Guerrillas in Spain," in *Guerrilla Reader,* ed. Laqueur, p. 159.

7. John J. Putnam, "Napoleon," *National Geographic* 161 (February 1982): 170–71.

8. Moorfield Storey and Marcial P. Lichauco, *The Conquest of the Philippines by the United States* (New York: G. P. Putnam's Sons, 1926), pp. 36–37.

9. James A. LeRoy, *The Americans in the Philippines: A History of the Conquest and First Years of Occupation with an Introductory Account of the Spanish Rule* (New York: Houghton Mifflin, 1914), II: 285n.; James H. Blount, *The American Occupation of the Philippines 1898–1912* (New York: G. P. Putnam's Sons, 1913), pp. 316–18.

10. John Womack, *Zapata and the Mexican Revolution* (New York: Knopf, 1969), pp. 3–5.

11. Ibid., pp. 78–82.

12. Ibid., p. 279.

13. Benedict J. Kerkvliet, *The Huk Rebellion: A Study of Peasant Revolt in the Philippines* (Berkeley and Los Angeles: University of California Press, 1977), pp. 1–60, *passim*.

14. Ibid., pp. 123–55.

15. Ibid., pp. 179, 188.

16. Ibid., pp. 219, 222.

17. Luis Taruc, *He Who Rides the Tiger* (London: Geoffrey Chapman, 1963), p. 93.

18. Ibid.; Kerkvliet, *Huk Rebellion*, pp. 213–14.

19. *Foreign Relations of the United States, 1950*, p. 1436.

20. Kerkvliet, *Huk Rebellion*, p. 239.

21. Albert Ravenholt, *The Philippines: A Young Republic on the Move* (Princeton, N.J.: D. Van Nostrand, 1962), p. 83.

22. Napoleon D. Valeriano and Charles T. R. Bohannan, *Counterguerrilla Operations: The Philippine Experience* (New York: Praeger, 1962), p. 106.

23. Ibid., pp. 239–40; Ravenholt, *Philippines*, p. 85.

24. Kerkvliet, *Huk Rebellion*, p. 238.

25. Taruc, *He Who Rides the Tiger*, pp. 134–36; Ravenholt, *Philippines*, pp. 85–86.

26. Rice, *Mao's Way*, p. 72.

27. Mao, *Selected Works*, I: 79, 92.

28. Stuart Schram, *Mao Tse-tung* (Baltimore: Penguin Books, 1966), p. 137.

29. Mao, *Selected Works*, I: 29, 97.

30. *Miscellany of Mao Tse-tung Thought, 1949–1968*, JPRS 61269-1 (Arlington, Va.: Joint Publications Research Service, 1974), I: 99.

31. Chalmers A. Johnson, *Peasant Nationalism and Communist Power: The Emergence of Revolutionary China 1937–1945* (Stanford: Stanford University Press, 1962), p. 146.

32. Ibid., p. 74.

33. Ibid., p. 89.

34. Ibid., p. 197 n. 20.

35. Edgar Snow, *Red Star over China* (New York: Random House, 1968), p. 411.

36. Mao, *Selected Works*, III: 269; Johnson, *Peasant Nationalism*, p. 192, n. 2.

37. Taruc, *He Who Rides the Tiger*, pp. 68–69.

38. Mao, *Selected Works*, I: 117–27.

39. Alistair Horne, *A Savage War of Peace: Algeria 1954–72* (New York: Viking, 1977), pp. 332, 535–37, 540–41.
40. Schram, *Mao Tse-tung,* pp. 151–53; Jerome Ch'en, *Mao and the Chinese Revolution* (New York: Oxford University Press, 1965), p. 173; Chang Kuo-t'ao, *The Rise of the Chinese Communist Party 1928–1938* (Lawrence: University Press of Kansas, 1972), pp. 165–68.
41. Horne, *Savage War,* pp. 260–61, 322–26.
42. Chang, *Rise of the Chinese Communist Party,* pp. 398–400.
43. *People's Daily,* 8 September 1977.
44. *China White Paper,* p. iii.
45. Stuart Schram, ed., *Chairman Mao Talks to the People: Talks and Letters, 1956–1971* (New York: Random House, 1974), p. 191.
46. Bernard B. Fall, *Street without Joy: Indochina at War, 1945–54* (Harrisburg, Pa.: Stackpole Books, 1961), pp. 27, 189–90; Allen S. Whiting, *The Chinese Calculus of Deterrence: India and Indochina* (Ann Arbor: University of Michigan Press, 1975), p. 170.
47. Oriana Fallaci, "China: The Sleeping Tiger Awakes," *San Francisco Chronicle,* 14 September 1980.

Chapter 4

1. Martín Luis Guzmán, *Memoirs of Pancho Villa,* trans. Virginia H. Taylor (Austin: University of Texas Press, 1965), pp. 102–20.
2. Womack, *Zapata,* pp. 178, 180–85, 221–22, 244.
3. William C. Westmoreland, *A Soldier Reports* (Garden City, N.Y.: Doubleday, 1976), p. 328.
4. Gabriel Kolko, *Anatomy of a War: Vietnam, the United States, and the Modern Historical Experience* (New York: Pantheon Books, 1985), p. 308; Stanley Karnow, *Vietnam: A History* (New York: Viking, 1983), pp. 526–27.
5. Karnow, *Vietnam,* p. 601.
6. Kolko, *Anatomy of a War,* p. 334.
7. Karnow, *Vietnam,* pp. 513–14.
8. Seymour M. Hersh, *The Price of Power: Kissinger in the Nixon White House* (New York: Summit Books, 1983), p. 298.
9. Rice, *Mao's Way,* p. 65; Whitson, *Chinese High Command,* pp. 263–64; Donald W. Klein and Anne B. Clark, *Biographic Dictionary of Chinese Communism, 1921–1965* (Cambridge, Mass.: Harvard University Press, 1971), II: 821.
10. Whitson, *Chinese High Command,* pp. 55–56.
11. Ibid., p. 275.

12. Rice, *Mao's Way*, p. 75.
13. Whitson, *Chinese High Command*, pp. 278–81.
14. Ibid., pp. 70, 159, 423.
15. Johnson, *Peasant Nationalism*, pp. 57–58.
16. Ibid., pp. 55–56.
17. Whitson, *Chinese High Command*, p. 74.
18. Johnson, *Peasant Nationalism*, pp. 158–59.
19. Whitson, *Chinese High Command*, p. 425.
20. Ibid., pp. 76, 82–83.
21. Clubb, *20th Century China*, pp. 254–55; *China White Paper*, p. 381.
22. Clubb, *20th Century China*, p. 257.
23. *China White Paper*, pp. 311–12.
24. Ibid., p. 312.
25. Whitson, *Chinese High Command*, pp. 181, 300, 319.
26. Ibid., pp. 180, 242–43.

Chapter 5

1. Mao, *Selected Works*, II: 136–37; Vo Nguyen Giap, *People's War, People's Army* (Hanoi: Foreign Languages Publishing House, 1961), pp. 46–47; Andrew F. Krepinevich, Jr., *The Army and Vietnam* (Baltimore: Johns Hopkins University Press, 1986), p. 7.
2. Douglas S. Blaufarb, *The Counterinsurgency Era: U.S. Doctrine and Performance, 1950 to the Present* (New York: Free Press, 1977), p. 80.
3. Krepinevich, *Army and Vietnam*, p. 149.
4. Thomas Edward Lawrence, "The Lessons of Arabia: The Arab Revolt of 1916–18," in *Guerrilla Reader*, ed. Laqueur, p. 131.
5. Russell F. Weigley, *The American Way of War: A History of United States Military Strategy and Policy* (New York: Macmillan, 1973), p. 77.
6. LeRoy, *Americans in the Philippines*, II: 125n.
7. Krepinevich, *Army and Vietnam*, pp. 78–79.
8. Taruc, *Born of the People*, pp. 108–15, 142; Valeriano and Bohannan, *Counterguerrilla Operations*, p. 23.
9. Horne, *Savage War*, p. 110.
10. Krepinevich, *Army in Vietnam*, p. 188; Guenter Lewy, *America in Vietnam* (New York: Oxford University Press, 1978), pp. 82–83.
11. Krepinevich, *Army in Vietnam*, p. 242; Lewy, *America in Vietnam*, pp. 82–83.
12. Douglas Kinnard, *The War Managers* (Hanover, N.H.: University Press of New England, 1977), p. 46.

13. *Pentagon Papers,* p. 372.
14. Stansfield Turner, "The War of Supplies," *New York Times,* 26 May 1982.
15. Charles Callwell, "The Dangers of Guerrilla War—1900," in *Guerrilla Reader,* ed. Laqueur, p. 116.
16. Kolko, *Anatomy of a War,* pp. 96, 131.
17. Lindsay, *Unknown War,* p. 6.
18. Clubb, *20th Century China,* p. 261.
19. Blount, *American Occupation of the Philippines,* pp. 378, 454, 457; Moorfield Storey and Marcial Lichauco, *The Conquest of the Philippines by the United States* (New York: G. P. Putnam's Sons, 1926), pp. 139–44; Leon Wolff, *Little Brown Brother: America's Forgotten Bid for Empire Which Cost 250,000 Lives* (New York, Longman, Green, 1961), pp. 354–57.
20. Storey and Lichauco, *Conquest of the Philippines,* p. 216; Stuart Creighton Miller, *"Benevolent Assimilation": The American Conquest of the Philippines, 1899–1903* (New Haven: Yale University Press, 1982), pp. 238–39, 243, 259.
21. Womack, *Zapata,* pp. 155–56; John K. Emerson, *The Japanese Thread: A Life in the U.S. Foreign Service* (New York: Holt, Rinehart & Winston, 1978), pp. 127–32.
22. Womack, *Zapata,* pp. 167–70, 183.
23. Blanch, *Sabres of Paradise,* pp. 299–301, 390–91.
24. Snow, *Red Star,* p. 188; Ch'en, *Mao and the Chinese Revolution,* p. 179; C. W. H. Wong, *New Life for Kiangsi* (Shanghai: New Life Publishing Company, 1931), photograph opposite p. 193.
25. Snow, *Red Star,* pp. 191–93; Agnes Smedley, *The Great Road* (New York: Monthly Review Press, 1956), p. 390; Whitson, *Chinese High Command,* pp. 278–81.
26. Thomas Packenham, *The Boer War* (New York: Random House, 1979), pp. 268–70, 274–83.
27. Tom Mangold and John Penycate, *The Tunnels of Cuchi* (New York: Random House, 1985), p. 39; Johnson, *Peasant Nationalism,* p. 58; Whitson, *Chinese High Command,* pp. 296, 343; Lindsay, *Unknown War,* pp. 5–6.
28. Lewy, *America in Vietnam,* p. 86.
29. Ibid., pp. 116–17; Blaufarb, *Counterinsurgency Era,* pp. 256–58; Krepinevich, *Army and Vietnam,* p. 175.
30. Westmoreland, *A Soldier Reports,* pp. 164–65.
31. Krepinevich, *Army and Vietnam,* p. 177.
32. Sheehan et al., eds., *Pentagon Papers,* pp. 601–02; Krepinevich, *Army and Vietnam,* pp. 175–76, 242–48.
33. Westmoreland, *A Soldier Reports,* p. 161.

34. Kinnard, *War Managers,* p. 43.
35. Lemière de Corvey, "Un Peu de fanatisme," in *Guerrilla Reader,* ed. Laqueur, p. 64.
36. Antoine Henri de Jomini, "National Wars," in *Guerrilla Reader,* ed. Laqueur, p. 44.
37. Miller, *"Benevolent Assimilation,"* pp. 213, 231–36, 259.
38. Robert B. Asprey, *War in the Shadows: The Guerrilla in History* (Garden City, N.Y.: Doubleday, 1975), I: 577–78.
39. Horne, *Savage War,* pp. 195–204.
40. In Yenan, in 1942, efforts to identify suspected Kuomintang infiltrators and other spies through the use of torture and other forms of pressure resulted in so great an epidemic of accusations and confessions that the top leaders, their credulity overtaxed, called off the search and provided an opportunity for people to repudiate their confessions and be rehabilitated. This is covered in James Pinckney Harrison, *The Long March to Power: A History of the Chinese Communist Party, 1921–1972* (New York: Praeger, 1972), pp. 341–42, and Wang Ming, *Mao's Betrayal* (Moscow: Progress Publishers, 1977), pp. 149–50. An earlier and somewhat similar case, the Futien Incident, is covered in my *Mao's Way,* pp. 67–69.
41. Horne, *Savage War,* pp. 206–7, 232–36, 416.
42. Mao, *Selected Works,* IV: 284.
43. Whitson, *Chinese High Command,* pp. 180, 242, 528 n. 151.
44. Klein and Clark, *Biographic Dictionary,* I: 622.
45. Georges Lefebvre, *Napoleon: From Tilsit to Waterloo, 1807–1815* (New York: Columbia University Press, 1969), pp. 29–30; Lemière de Corvey, "Un Peu de fanatisme," in *Guerrilla Reader,* ed. Laqueur, pp. 64–65; Marx and Engels, "Guerrillas in Spain," in ibid., p. 159.
46. Thomas P. Anderson, *Politics in Central America: Guatemala, El Salvador, Honduras, and Nicaragua* (New York: Praeger, 1982), p. 69; Raymond Bonner, *Weakness and Deceit: U.S. Policy and El Salvador* (New York: Times Books, 1984), pp. 96–97.
47. Martin Van Creveld, *Command in War* (Cambridge, Mass.: Harvard University Press, 1985), p. 246.
48. Ibid., 249.
49. Lewy, *America in Vietnam,* pp. 56–63; Krepinevich, *Army in Vietnam,* pp. 166–67.
50. Blaufarb, *Counterinsurgency Era,* pp. 245–46.
51. Lewy, *America in Vietnam,* p. 272; Pike, *Viet Cong,* pp. 210–11.
52. Blaufarb, *Counterinsurgency Era,* p. 246; Kolko, *Anatomy of a War,* p. 330; William Colby and Peter Forbath, *Honorable Men: My Life in the CIA* (New York: Simon & Schuster, 1978), p. 268.
53. Kolko, *Anatomy of a War,* p. 388; Colby, *Honorable Men,* p. 234.

54. Blaufarb, *Counterinsurgency Era*, p. 247.
55. Colby, *Honorable Men*, p. 272; Lewy, *America in Vietnam*, pp. 280–81.
56. Krepinevich, *Army and Vietnam*, pp. 228–29; Blaufarb, *Counterinsurgency Era*, p. 247; Lewy, *America in Vietnam*, pp. 281–85.
57. Karnow, *Vietnam*, p. 534.
58. Kolko, *Anatomy of a War*, p. 330.
59. Ibid., 186; Pike, *Viet Cong*, p. 137 n. 2.
60. Karnow, *Vietnam*, p. 610; Westmoreland, *A Soldier Reports*, pp. 206, 272.
61. Page Smith, *A New Age Now Begins: A People's History of the American Revolution* (New York: McGraw-Hill, 1976), p. 453.
62. Baddeley, *Russian Conquest*, p. 138.
63. Blanch, *Sabres of Paradise*, p. 24.
64. Baddeley, *Russian Conquest*, p. 144.
65. Ibid., pp. 135, 245.
66. Ibid., pp. xxxvi, 153.
67. Ibid., p. 244.
68. Blanch, *Sabres of Paradise*, p. 253.
69. Ibid., p. 153.
70. Baddeley, *Russian Conquest*, p. 446.
71. Blanch, *Sabres of Paradise*, pp. 300–301.
72. Ibid., p. 450; Richard Bernstein, "Remaking Afghanistan in the Soviet Image," *New York Times Magazine*, 24 March 1985, p. 32.
73. René Bittard des Portes, *Charette et la guerre de Vendée* (Paris: Émile-Paul, 1902), pp. 294–96.
74. Ibid., p. 349.
75. Ibid., 495–96; *Encyclopedia Britannica*, 1974 ed., s.v. "Vendée, Wars of the."
76. Bittard des Portes, *Charette*, pp. 511, 552 n. 2; *New Columbia Encyclopedia*, s.v. "Vendée."
77. Franklin Mark Osanka, ed., *Modern Guerrilla Warfare: Fighting Communist Guerrilla Movements, 1941–1961* (Glencoe, Ill.: Free Press of Glencoe, 1962), p. xxi.
78. Valeriano and Bohannan, *Counterguerrilla Operations*, p. 97.
79. Ibid., pp. 129–31.
80. Kerkvliet, *Huk Rebellion*, pp. 237–42.
81. Laqueur, ed., *Guerrilla Reader*, p. 6.
82. Jomini, "National Wars," in ibid., p. 44; David G. Chandler, *Dictionary of the Napoleonic Wars* (New York: Macmillan, 1979), pp. 429–30.
83. Horne, *Savage War*, p. 468.
84. Kinnard, *War Managers*, p. 162.

85. U. Alexis Johnson, *The Right Hand of Power* (Englewood Cliffs, N.J.: Prentice-Hall, 1984), pp. 632–33.

Chapter 6

1. Helen H. Robbins, *Our First Ambassador to China* (New York: Dutton, 1908), pp. 376–77, 384–85, quoting from the China Journal of Lord Macartney.
2. *China White Paper*, pp. 19–20.
3. *The Memoirs of Prince Fumimaro Konoye,* trans. Okuyama Service (Tokyo: Asahi Shimbun, 20–31 December 1945), pp. 6–12, 23; Robert J. C. Butow, *Tojo and the Coming of the War* (Stanford: Stanford University Press, 1961), pp. 229, 260n.
4. Konoye, *Memoirs*, pp. 6–13.
5. Ibid., p. 23; Butow, *Tojo*, pp. 241–42.
6. Butow, *Tojo*, pp. 230–31, 260n.
7. *China White Paper*, p. 25.
8. Butow, *Tojo*, p. 198.
9. Fall, *Street without Joy*, pp. 21–22.
10. Konoye, *Memoirs*, pp. 26, 36–37; Barbara W. Tuchman, *Stillwell and the American Experience in China, 1911–45* (New York: Macmillan, 1971), pp. 223–24.
11. Courtney Browne, *Tojo: The Last Banzai* (New York: Holt, Rinehart & Winston, 1967), pp. 91–92.
12. Butow, *Tojo*, pp. 236–37.
13. Ibid., pp. 248–49.
14. Ibid., p. 237; Konoye, *Memoirs*, pp. 4, 55–56.
15. Konoye, *Memoirs*, pp. 48–49; Butow, *Tojo*, pp. 248–55.
16. Konoye, *Memoirs*, p. 50.
17. Butow, *Tojo*, pp. 170–73.
18. Ibid., pp. 256–58.
19. Ibid., pp. 263–85.
20. Konoye, *Memoirs*, p. 61; Edwin O. Reischauer, *Japan: The Story of a Nation* (New York: Knopf, 1981), p. 148; Edwin O. Reischauer, *The Japanese* (Cambridge, Mass.: Harvard University Press, 1977), p. 92.
21. Butow, *Tojo*, p. 301.
22. Ibid., pp. 319, 326, 333–34.
23. Ibid., pp. 121–22.
24. Browne, *Tojo*, pp. 124–27.
25. Reischauer, *Japanese*, pp. 106–7; Reischauer, *Japan*, pp. 229–31.

26. Horne, *Savage War,* pp. 34, 35.

27. Ibid., p. 94.

28. Ibid., pp. 85, 129.

29. Ibid., p. 162.

30. Georgiana G. Stevens, *Egypt Yesterday and Today* (New York: Holt, Rinehart & Winston, 1963), pp. 207–8; *New Columbia Encyclopedia,* s.v. "Suez Canal."

31. *New Columbia Encyclopedia,* s.v. "Suez Canal"; Horne, *Savage War,* pp. 157, 161–64.

32. Horne, *Savage War,* pp. 263–64.

33. Alf Andrew Heggoy, *Insurgency and Counterinsurgency in Algeria* (Bloomington: Indiana University Press, 1972), p. 240.

34. Horne, *Savage War,* pp. 249–50.

35. Ibid., p. 169.

36. Ibid., pp. 174–82.

37. Ibid., pp. 283–93.

38. Ibid., pp. 293–98.

39. Ibid., pp. 308–9.

40. Ibid., pp. 305–6, 331, 337, 340–41, 382.

41. Ibid., pp. 338–39; Heggoy, *Insurgency,* pp. 214–17.

42. Horne, *Savage War,* pp. 310–11.

43. Ibid., pp. 340, 344.

44. Ibid., pp. 353–74.

45. Ibid., pp. 428–33.

46. Ibid., p. 426.

47. Ibid., p. 454.

48. Ibid., pp. 441, 448–62.

49. Ibid., pp. 480–81.

50. Ibid., pp. 232, 239.

51. Ibid., p. 234.

52. Ibid., pp. 183, 201–3, 231–32.

53. Ibid., p. 196.

54. Ibid., pp. 176, 203–4, 231–32.

55. Ibid., p. 499.

56. Ibid., p. 467.

57. Ibid., p. 441.

58. Ibid., pp. 500–504.

59. Ibid., pp. 499–500.

60. Ibid., pp. 543–44.

61. Ibid., p. 293.

62. Wolff, *Little Brown Brother,* pp. 261–62; Blount, *American Occupation,* pp. 219–20.
63. Blount, *American Occupation,* pp. 219–20.
64. LeRoy, *Americans in the Philippines,* II: 49–51.
65. Ibid., pp. 49–55, 125n.
66. Miller, *Benevolent Assimilation,* pp. 129, 232.
67. LeRoy, *Americans in the Philippines,* II: 56–64; Dino J. Caterini, "Repeating Ourselves: The Philippine Insurrection and the Vietnam War," *Foreign Service Journal,* December 1977, pp. 11–17, 31–32.
68. W. Cameron Forbes, *The Philippine Islands* (Cambridge, Mass.: Harvard University Press, 1945), p. 66; Storey and Lichuaco, *Conquest of the Philippines,* p. 69.
69. Miller, *Benevolent Assimilation,* pp. 220, 222.
70. Blount, *American Occupation,* pp. 104, 480–87.
71. Ibid., pp. 412, 501.
72. Ibid., pp. 280, 331.
73. Ibid., p. 450.
74. Karnow, *Vietnam,* pp. 561–62; Maxwell D. Taylor, *Swords and Plowshares* (New York: W. W. Norton, 1972), pp. 390–91; Herbert Y. Schandler, *The Unmaking of a President: Lyndon Johnson and Vietnam* (Princeton: Princeton University Press, 1977), p. 263.
75. Schandler, *Unmaking of a President,* pp. 268–87.
76. *Time,* 28 June 1971, p. 15.
77. *New York Times,* 21 June 1979.
78. Marvin Kalb and Elie Abel, *Roots of Involvement: The United States in Asia, 1784–1971* (New York: W. W. Norton, 1971), p. 233.
79. Whiting, *Chinese Calculus,* p. xix.
80. Hersh, *Price of Power,* p. 60.
81. Ibid., pp. 54–63; William Shawcross, *Sideshow: Kissinger, Nixon and the Destruction of Cambodia* (New York: Simon & Schuster, 1979), pp. 31–32.
82. Shawcross, *Sideshow,* pp. 33, 106; Hersh, *Price of Power,* pp. 86–87, 93–94; H. R. Haldeman, *The Ends of Power* (New York: Times Books, 1978), pp. 100–101.
83. Shawcross, *Sideshow,* pp. 126, 163.
84. Hersh, *Price of Power,* pp. 199–200.
85. Shawcross, *Sideshow,* p. 179.
86. Haldeman, *Ends of Power,* pp. 104–5; Hersh, *Price of Power,* pp. 208–9.
87. Hersh, *Price of Power,* p. 209; John W. Dean III, *Blind Ambition: The White House Years* (New York: Simon & Schuster, 1976), pp. 36–37.

88. Dave Richard Palmer, *Summons of the Trumpet: A History of the Vietnam War from a Military Man's Viewpoint* (New York: Ballantine Books, 1978), pp. 308–9; Hersh, *Price of Power,* p. 308.

89. Karnow, *Vietnam,* p. 632.

90. Hersh, *Price of Power,* p. 390.

91. Haldeman, *Ends of Power,* p. 79.

92. Bob Woodward and Carl Bernstein, *The Final Days* (New York: Avon, 1976), pp. 333, 514.

Chapter 7

1. John Kenneth Galbraith, "The Strategic Mind," *New York Review of Books,* 12 October 1978.

2. *New York Times,* 21 April 1987.

3. Henry Kissinger, *Years of Upheaval* (Boston: Little, Brown, 1982), p. 102.

4. Richard E. Neustadt and Ernest R. May, *Thinking in Time: The Uses of History for Decision-Makers* (New York: Free Press, 1986), p. 7.

5. George W. Ball, *The Past Has Another Pattern: Memoirs* (New York: W. W. Norton, 1982), pp. 396–97.

6. Neustadt and May, *Thinking in Time,* pp. 87, 161–63.

7. Kalb and Abel, *Roots of Involvement,* pp. 90–91.

8. Ambrose, *Eisenhower,* pp. 173, 210.

9. Neustadt and May, *Thinking in Time,* p. 86.

10. *San Francisco Chronicle,* 12 February 1987.

11. Tom Wicker, "Not So Neat War," *New York Times,* 11 June 1985; Stephen Engelberg, "U.S. and the Nicaraguan Rebels: Six Years of Questions and Contradictions," ibid., 3 May 1987. See also the account of testimony of Elliott Abrams in ibid., 3 June 1987.

12. *New York Times,* 30 June 1985.

13. Krepinevich, *Army and Vietnam,* pp. 269–70.

14. *Pentagon Papers,* p. xx.

nese military's plans to go to war against U.S. and Great Britain, 121–26

Korean War, as analogy for Vietnam, 152

Krepinevich, Andrew F., Jr.: on escalation from counterinsurgency to conventional warfare, 154

Kunming, 123

Laird, Melvin, 147
Lane, Arthur Bliss, 31
Lansdale, Edward G., 9
Lao Dong, 107
Laos, extension of Vietnam War to, 145, 147
Latifundia, 21–22
Lava, José, 68, 75
Lawrence, T. E., on irregular forces for wars of detachment, 92
Lemière de Corvey, J. F. A., 63
Lines of communication, inability of guerrillas to defend, 55
Lodge, Henry Cabot, 42, 45
Logistical requirements for conversion from guerrilla warfare to conventional operations, 79–80, 88
Logistics: Chinese Communist, as based on populace of broad countryside, 86–88; Chinese Nationalist, as based on centers and lines of communication, 86; as dominating strategy, 95; of guerrilla forces, as largely dependent on captures, 53, 87, 88
Long March, 76, 84, 99

MacArthur, Arthur (general), 65
MacArthur, Douglas (general), 86
Macartney, Lord, 120
McGarr, Lionel C. (general), 12
Machado, Gerardo, 22
McKinley, William, 140

McNaughton, John T., 155
MACV (U.S. Military Assistance Command, Vietnam), 93, 106
Magsaysay, Ramon, 9–10, 116; appointed secretary of defense, 69; Huk rebellion suppressed by, 69–70; military and political counterinsurgency measures combined by, 113–14
Malaya, Emergency in, 59, 116
Managua, and 1972 earthquake, 34
Manchuria, 86
Mao Zedong, 13, 55, 90, 105; disobedience of to Party Center, 75, 76, 82; on incompatibility of guerrilla operations and unified, capitalist economies, 56; as revolutionary thinker, 57
Mao's Way, 16
Marshall, George C. (general): China mission of, 5–7; on democracies as unsuited to fighting seven-year wars, 118–19; and U.S. military involvement in China's civil war, 7–8
Martínez de Campos, Arsenio (general), 19, 20
Marxist-Leninist parties, stress on organization by, 66
Mass organizations, Chinese Communist: in Jiangxi, 70; in North China during Sino-Japanese War, 73
Massu, Jacques (general), 104, 137
Matsuoka, Yosuke, 122
May, Ernest R., 151
Maya Indians, in Guatemalan insurgency, 49
Mayorga, Silvio: Marxist co-founder of FSLN, 33; killed, 33
Meiji, 126
Mejía Victores, Oscar Humberto (general), 50
Mendès-France, Pierre, 132
Mendieta, Carlos, 27